First World War
and Army of Occupation
War Diary
France, Belgium and Germany

37 DIVISION
112 Infantry Brigade
Bedfordshire Regiment
6th Battalion
30 July 1915 - 30 June 1918

WO95/2537/3

The Naval & Military Press Ltd
www.nmarchive.com
Published in association with The National Archives

Published by

The Naval & Military Press Ltd

Unit 10 Ridgewood Industrial Park,

Uckfield, East Sussex,

TN22 5QE England

Tel: +44 (0) 1825 749494

www.naval-military-press.com

www.nmarchive.com

This diary has been reprinted in facsimile from the original. Any imperfections are inevitably reproduced and the quality may fall short of modern type and cartographic standards.

© **Crown Copyright**
Images reproduced by permission of The National Archives, London, England, 2015.

Contents

Document type	Place/Title	Date From	Date To
Heading	WO95/2537/3		
Heading	37th Division 112th Infy Bde 6th Bn Bedfordshire Regt Aug 1915-1918 Jun Disbanded		
Heading	112th Inf. Bde. 37th Div. Battn. Disembarked Havre From England 31.7.15 War Diary. 6th Battn. The Bedfordshire Regiment. August (30.7.15 To 31.8.15) 1915		
War Diary	Ludgershall	30/07/1915	30/07/1915
War Diary	Havre	31/07/1915	01/08/1915
War Diary	Zutkerke	02/08/1915	02/08/1915
War Diary	Argues	04/08/1915	04/08/1915
War Diary	Hazebrouck	05/08/1915	10/08/1915
War Diary	Locre	11/08/1915	19/08/1915
War Diary	Hazebrouck	21/08/1915	24/08/1915
War Diary	Godewaersvelde	26/08/1915	26/08/1915
War Diary	Orville	27/08/1915	31/08/1915
Heading	112th Inf. Bde. 37th Div. War Diary. 6th Battn. The Bedfordshire Regiment. September 1915		
War Diary	Orville.	01/09/1915	04/09/1915
War Diary	Fonquvillers.	05/09/1915	11/09/1915
War Diary	Humber Camp.	12/09/1915	15/09/1915
War Diary	Bienvillers.	16/09/1915	21/09/1915
War Diary	Hannescamp	22/09/1915	30/09/1915
Heading	112th Inf. Bde. 37th Div. War Diary. 6th Battn. The Bedfordshire Regiment. October 1915		
War Diary	Humber Camp.	01/10/1915	08/10/1915
War Diary	Bienvilliers	09/10/1915	14/10/1915
War Diary	Hannescamps.	15/10/1915	20/10/1915
War Diary	Bienvilliers.	21/10/1915	27/10/1915
War Diary	Saint Amand.	28/10/1915	31/10/1915
Heading	112th Inf. Bde. 37th Div. War Diary 6th Battn. The Bedfordshire Regiment. November 1915		
War Diary	Saint Amand	01/11/1915	01/11/1915
War Diary	Bienvillers.	02/11/1915	07/11/1915
War Diary	Hannescamp.	08/11/1915	14/11/1915
War Diary	Humber Camp.	15/11/1915	25/11/1915
War Diary	Bienvillers.	26/11/1915	29/11/1915
War Diary	Hannescamp	30/11/1915	30/11/1915
Heading	112th Inf. Bde. 37th Div. War Diary 6th Battn. The Bedfordshire Regiment. December 1915		
War Diary	Humber Camp	09/11/1915	20/11/1915
War Diary	Bienvillers.	21/11/1915	26/11/1915
War Diary	Hannescamp	27/11/1915	02/12/1915
War Diary	Bienvillers	03/12/1915	05/12/1915
War Diary	Hannescamp	06/12/1915	08/12/1915
Heading	112th Inf. Bde. 37th Division 1/6th Battalion. Bedfordshire Regiment. January 1916		
War Diary	Hannescamp.	01/01/1916	01/01/1916
War Diary	Humber Camp.	02/01/1916	13/01/1916
War Diary	Bienvillers.	14/01/1916	19/01/1916

Type	Description	Start	End
War Diary	Hannescamp	20/01/1916	25/01/1916
War Diary	Humbercamp.	26/01/1916	31/01/1916
Heading	112th Inf. Bde. 37th Div.1/6th Battalion Bedfordshire Regiment. February 1916		
War Diary	Humbercamp.	01/02/1916	05/02/1916
War Diary	Bienvillers.	06/02/1916	09/02/1916
War Diary	Hannescamp.	10/02/1916	13/02/1916
War Diary	St. Amand.	14/02/1916	15/02/1916
War Diary	Trenches.	16/02/1916	22/02/1916
War Diary	St. Amand.	23/02/1916	29/02/1916
Heading	112th Inf. Bde. 37th Div. 1/6th. Battalion Bedford Regiment March 1916		
War Diary	Saint Amand	01/03/1916	01/03/1916
War Diary	Pommier.	02/03/1916	06/03/1916
War Diary	Hannescamps.	07/03/1916	12/03/1916
War Diary	Bienvilliers.	13/03/1916	19/03/1916
War Diary	Humbercamps	20/03/1916	31/03/1916
Heading	112th Brigade. 37th Division. 1/6th Battalion Bedford Regiment April 1916		
War Diary	Humbercamps.	01/04/1916	09/04/1916
War Diary	Sus-St-Leger.	10/04/1916	30/04/1916
Heading	112th Inf. Bde. 37th Div. 1/6th Battalion Bedford Regiment May 1916		
Heading	D.A.G. G.H.Q. 3rd Echelon Base War Diary Of 6 "S" Bn Bedfordshire Regt Period 1st to 31st May		
Miscellaneous	Absor in 1/1 Herts		
War Diary		01/05/1916	30/05/1916
Heading	112th Brigade. 37th Division. Went With 112th Brigade To 34th Division 5th July 1916-Rejoined 37th Division 21st August 1916 1/6th Battalion Bedford Regiment June 1916		
War Diary		01/06/1916	30/06/1916
Heading	112th Brigade 37th Division. 34th Division From 5th July. Transferred With 112th Brigade From 37th To 34th Division 5th July 1916 1/6th Battalion Bedfordshire Regiment July 1916		
War Diary	Bienvillers.	01/07/1916	31/07/1916
War Diary	112th Brigade. 34th Division Till 22nd August Rejoined 37th Division 22nd August 1916 1/6th Battalion Bedfordshire Regiment August 1916 Report On Attack 9th August 1916 Attached.		
War Diary		01/08/1916	31/08/1916
Miscellaneous	Messages And Signals 112th Bde.		
Miscellaneous	Operation Orders M. Lt. Col. Edwards Commdg 6th Bedf R.	08/08/1916	08/08/1916
Heading	112th Brigade. 37th Division. 1/6th Battalion Bedford Regiment September 1916		
War Diary		01/09/1916	05/09/1916
War Diary		02/09/1916	18/09/1916
War Diary		15/09/1916	30/09/1916
War Diary	112th Brigade. 37th Division. 1/6th Battalion Bedford Regiment October 1916		
War Diary		01/10/1916	31/10/1916
Heading	112th 37th Division. 1/6th Battalion Bedford Regiment November 1916		
War Diary	Sarton	01/11/1916	30/11/1916

Heading	112th Inf. Bde. 37th Div. 1/6th Battalion Bedford Regiment December 1916		
War Diary		01/12/1916	30/12/1916
Heading	War Diary Of 6th Bedfords. January 1917. Vol 18		
War Diary		01/01/1917	29/01/1917
Heading	War Diary 6th Bedford Vol 19 Feb 1917		
War Diary		01/02/1917	28/02/1917
War Diary	Loos.	01/03/1917	31/03/1917
Heading	War Diary For April 1917 6th Bedfordshire Regt. Vol. 21		
War Diary	Etree-Wamin	02/04/1917	28/04/1917
Operation(al) Order(s)	Operation Order By Lieut Col F.M. Edwards Commdg 6th "S" Bn Bedfordshire Regt. 7-4-17	07/04/1917	07/04/1917
Miscellaneous	Operation Orders By Lt Col F.H. Edwards Commdg 6th Bedfordshire Regt.	08/04/1917	08/04/1917
Miscellaneous	Diary of events April 9th-12th 1917	09/04/1917	09/04/1917
Map	J. Corps T.S. No. M. 12 (a) (b) Trench Map 51 B. N.W.		
Heading	War Diary 6th (S) Bn Bedfordshire Regt. Vol. III No. V Vol 22		
War Diary	Berlencourt	01/05/1917	15/05/1917
War Diary	Montenescourt	18/05/1917	18/05/1917
War Diary	Tilloy	19/05/1917	19/05/1917
War Diary	Support Trenches.	20/05/1917	23/05/1917
War Diary	Frontline Trenches.	24/05/1917	24/05/1917
War Diary	Trenches	25/05/1917	28/06/1917
War Diary	Achicourt.	29/05/1917	31/05/1917
Heading	War Diary 6th Bedfords June 1917 Vol 23		
War Diary	Duisans.	01/06/1917	03/06/1917
War Diary	Izel	04/06/1917	08/06/1917
War Diary	Delette	09/06/1917	25/06/1917
War Diary	Locre.	28/06/1917	29/06/1917
War Diary	Kemmel.	30/06/1917	30/06/1917
War Diary	War Diary July 1917 6th Bedfords. Vol 24		
War Diary	Baileeul.	01/07/1917	10/07/1917
War Diary	Kemmel Hill	11/07/1917	19/07/1917
War Diary	Trenches.	20/07/1917	25/07/1917
War Diary	Kemmel Hill	26/07/1917	26/07/1917
War Diary	Bailleul.	27/07/1917	30/07/1917
Heading	War Diary 6th Bedfords Aug 1917 Vol 25		
War Diary	Bailleul.	01/08/1917	02/08/1917
War Diary	Kemmel.	03/08/1917	07/08/1917
War Diary	Trenches.	08/08/1917	15/08/1917
War Diary	Siege Farm.	16/08/1917	21/08/1917
War Diary	Trenches.	22/08/1917	27/08/1917
War Diary	Chinese Wall.	28/08/1917	29/08/1917
Heading	War Diary 6th Bedfords Septr 1917 Vol 26		
War Diary	Kemmel Shelters.	01/09/1917	02/09/1917
War Diary	Trenches.	03/09/1917	11/09/1917
War Diary	Westoutre.	12/09/1917	19/09/1917
War Diary	R.E. Farm.	20/09/1917	21/09/1917
War Diary	Westoutre	22/09/1917	22/09/1917
War Diary	Trenches.	23/09/1917	27/09/1917
War Diary	R.E. Farm.	28/09/1917	28/09/1917
War Diary	Bois Carre.	29/09/1917	29/09/1917

Heading	War Diary Of 6th (Service) Battalion Bedfordshire Regiment. From 1st October 1917 To 31st October 1917 Volume 27		
War Diary	Bois Carre	01/10/1917	04/10/1917
War Diary	Trenches.	04/10/1917	09/10/1917
War Diary	Little Kemmel	10/10/1917	12/10/1917
War Diary	West Outre.	13/10/1917	14/10/1917
War Diary	West Outre and Ypres	15/10/1917	18/10/1917
War Diary	West Outre	19/10/1917	23/10/1917
War Diary	Berthen.	24/10/1917	26/10/1917
War Diary	Locre.	27/10/1917	07/11/1917
War Diary	Bois Confluent	08/11/1917	08/11/1917
War Diary	Line	09/11/1917	17/11/1917
War Diary	Bois Confluent	18/11/1917	24/11/1917
War Diary	Tournai Camp.	25/11/1917	04/12/1917
War Diary	Trenches.	05/12/1917	12/12/1917
War Diary	Spoilbank.	13/12/1917	20/12/1917
War Diary	Curragh Camp	21/12/1917	31/12/1917
War Diary	Trenches,	01/01/1917	05/01/1917
War Diary	Tournai Camp.	06/01/1917	10/01/1917
War Diary	Sercus.	11/01/1917	21/01/1917
War Diary	Maida Camp.	22/01/1917	31/01/1917
Heading	Confidential War Diary. Of 6th Battalion Bedfordshire Regt. From February 1st 1918 To February 28th 1918 Volume. 31		
War Diary	Maida Camp	01/02/1918	04/02/1918
War Diary	Billets	05/02/1918	05/02/1918
War Diary	Heuringhen	06/02/1918	14/02/1918
War Diary	Heuringhen Camp.	15/02/1918	15/02/1918
War Diary	Trenches.	17/02/1918	21/02/1918
War Diary	Maida Camp.	22/02/1918	26/02/1918
War Diary	Trenches.	27/02/1918	28/02/1918
Heading	War Diary Of 6th Bedford Regt. For March 1918 Volume XXXI Vol 32		
War Diary	Front Line	01/03/1918	04/03/1918
War Diary	Trenches.	05/03/1918	11/03/1918
War Diary	Maida Camp	12/03/1918	16/03/1918
War Diary	Trenches.	17/03/1918	24/03/1918
War Diary	Malplaquet Camp.	25/03/1918	27/03/1918
War Diary	Borre	28/03/1918	28/03/1918
War Diary	Mondicourt	29/03/1918	30/03/1918
War Diary	Couin.	31/03/1918	31/03/1918
Heading	112th Inf. Bde. 37th Div. War Diary 6th Battn. The Bedfordshire Regiment. April 1918		
Heading	Confidential War Diary. Of 6th Bedford Regt. From 1st April To 30th April 1918 Volume XXXII Vol 33		
War Diary	Trenches.	01/04/1918	09/04/1918
War Diary	Gommecourt.	10/04/1918	12/04/1918
War Diary	Trenches.	13/04/1918	16/04/1918
War Diary	Bois De Warnimont.	17/04/1918	24/04/1918
War Diary	Fonquevillers.	25/04/1918	30/04/1918
Heading	Training Cadre 39th Division 116th Infy Bde 6th Bn Bedford Regt May-June 1918		
War Diary	Line	01/05/1918	17/05/1918
War Diary	Louvencourt.	18/05/1918	21/05/1918
War Diary	Nielles	22/05/1918	30/05/1918

War Diary   Nielles. Les. Ardres   01/06/1918 30/06/1918

37TH DIVISION
112TH INFY BDE

6TH BN BEDFORDSHIRE REGT
AUG 1915 - APR 1918
1918 JULY

DISBANDED

112th Inf.Bde.
37th Div.

Battn. disembarked
Havre from England
31.7.15.

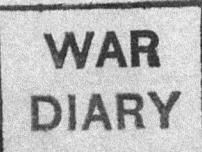

6th BATTN. THE BEDFORDSHIRE REGIMENT.

A U G U S T

(30.7.15 to 31.8.15)

1 9 1 5

Army Form C. 2118.

INTELLIGENCE SUMMARY.
(Erase heading not required.)

Instructions regarding War Diaries and Intelligence Summaries are contained in F. S. Regs., Part II. and the Staff Manual respectively. Title pages will be prepared in manuscript.

Place	Date	Hour	Summary of Events and Information	Remarks and references to Appendices
Lydd, and Gd	30.7.15	7 a.m.	The Battalion entrained at Lydd and Gd station. Transport under command of Major B.P. Newbolt. B & C Companies under command of Lt Col P.E. Barclay & A & D Companies under command of Major R.L. Haggett at 11 a.m. Detrained at Southampton. The Battalion embarked. Transport embarked on the Empress Queen at 6.30 p.m.	
Havre	31.7.15	7.30 a.m.	The Battalion disembarked and marched to No 5 Camp	
Havre	1.8.15	5.30 p.m.	The Battalion entrained at the Gare de Marchandise	
Zuytpeene	2.8.15	8.30	Detrained at Cauderry at 8.30 a.m. and marched to Zuytpeene. m.6. Billets	
Arques	4.8.15		Marched from Zuytpeene at 8 a.m. joined 112th Brigade at Nordausque and reached Arques at 4.45 p.m	
Hazebrouck	5.8.15		Marched from Arques at 8 a.m and reached Hazebrouck at 1.15 p.m. and went into billets	
Hazebrouck	8.8.15		The Battalion was inspected by Lt. General Sir H. Plumer Commanding the 2nd Army.	
Hazebrouck	10.8.15	6 a.m.	A detachment of 557 o.r. & 17 Officers under Command of Major B.P. Newbolt marched to LOCRE.	
Locre	11.8.15		The Detacht commenced digging Reserve Trenches under an Engineer Officer about 1 mile N. of KEMMEL	
Locre	19.8.15		Whilst digging at night 2nd Lt G.A. SMITH-MASTERS advanced out of the Trenches and was shot dead. It is supposed by a Sniper.	
Hazebrouck	21.8.15		Major B.P. NEWBOLT returned in order to take over Command of the Battalion.	
Hazebrouck	22.8.15		Lt Col H.F. BARCLAY relinquished command and left for ARMENTIERES.	

T2134. Wt. W708—776. 500000. 4/15. Sir J. C. & S.

INTELLIGENCE SUMMARY.

(Erase heading not required.)

Instructions regarding War Diaries and Intelligence Summaries are contained in F.S. Regs. Part II. and the Staff Manual respectively. Title pages will be prepared in manuscript.

Place	Date	Hour	Summary of Events and Information	Remarks and references to Appendices
Hazebrouck	24.8.15	1.30pm	The Battn proceeded by march Route to GODEWAERSVELDE and arrived in Billets there at 4.30pm when Lt Colonel R.T. TOKE (1st Watch Rgt) joined and proceeded to take over command of the Battn	
Godewaersvelde	26.8.15	2.33am	The Battn entrained & proceeded by rail to DOULLENS arriving there 9.30 a.m. then proceeded by march route to Billets at ORVILLE.	
ORVILLE	27.8.15		Very hot day. Battn engaged in settling into billets & billet lines etc Grds	
"	28.8.29		Battn engaged in route marches & Parades	
"	30.8.15		Battn inspected by Gen. Sir C. Monro Commdr 3rd Army.	
"	31.8.15		All officers of Battn instructed in bombing	

31.8.15

R.T. TOKE Lt Col
Commdg 6th Batt. The Buckinghamshire Regt

112th Inf.Bde.
37th Div.

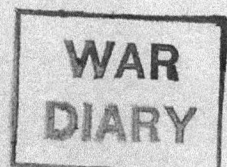

6th BATTN. THE BEDFORDSHIRE REGIMENT.

S E P T E M B E R

1 9 1 5

WAR DIARY
or
INTELLIGENCE SUMMARY.
(Erase heading not required.)

Instructions regarding War Diaries and Intelligence Summaries are contained in F.S. Regs., Part II. and the Staff Manual respectively. Title pages will be prepared in manuscript.

Army Form C. 2118.

Hour, Date, Place		Summary of Events and Information	Remarks and references to Appendices
ORVILLE.	1.9.15	In billets - Route march.	
"	2.9.15	" " "	
"	3.9.15	" " Company Bombers - Bomb practice with guncotton.	
"	4.9.15	" Company Bazaar about to travel	
FONQUEVILLERS	5.9.15	Marched to FONQUEVILLERS. - A. & B. Coys. went into the trenches for instruction under 143rd Brigade. Trench very quiet.	
"	6.9.15	2 Coys. in the trenches. - 2 Coys. in village. Daily return of trench casualties. Pte Hattaway & Pte Castle B. Coy. wounded.	
"	7.9.15	As above German very quiet. Our artillery	
"	8.9.15	Quiet on German front. Little reply.	
"	9.9.15	German fire = arise to open our large dugouts. Some about 6 shrapnel but our fire short. C. & D. Coys. went into the trenches. L/Cpl Sharp, Pte Burden withdrew however.	
"	10.9.15	Our Artillery fired on the German all morning. Our Machine Gun fire during the night.	
"	11.9.15	Left FONQUEVILLERS - marched to HUMBERCAMP & joined the 112th Brigade.	

INTELLIGENCE SUMMARY.

(Erase heading not required.)

Instructions regarding War Diaries and Intelligence Summaries are contained in F.S. Regs., Part II and the Staff Manual respectively. Title pages will be prepared in manuscript.

Hour, Date, Place	Summary of Events and Information	Remarks and references to Appendices
HUMBERCAMP. 12.9.15	In Billets. Men employed digging a flume round village. Billet hut very good.	
13.9.15	As above. Very hot.	
14.9.15	As above. Very hot.	
15.9.15	Left HUMBERCAMP. Marched to BIENVILLERS. Billets very good.	
BIENVILLERS. 16.9.15	Working parties out all day. Right Halves on fatigue. Line trenches at HANNESCAMP.	
17.9.15	Our artillery active but very little reply from enemy. Heavy bombardment going on in direction of ARRAS.	
18.9.15	Working parties out digging all day & night.	
19.9.15	German aircraft active but driven off by our airmen.	
20.9.15	Our artillery active all day but very little reply from German guns. The only small white bangs.	
21.9.15	Moved to HANNESCAMP and relieved Loyal North Lancs in trenches. German sent over a good many shells & some to straf(e) from start about 9.15 no damage done.	

WAR DIARY
or
INTELLIGENCE SUMMARY.
(Erase heading not required.)

Instructions regarding War Diaries and Intelligence Summaries are contained in F. S. Regs., Part II. and the Staff Manual respectively. Title pages will be prepared in manuscript.

Hour, Date, Place	Summary of Events and Information	Remarks and references to Appendices
HANNESCAMP 22.9.15	Our Artillery fired all day. On German trenches and dugouts. German Shelled POMMIER. Trenches fairly quiet, but Enemy have Dugout our Support trenches hit any in some places.	
" 23.9.15	Our Artillery again very active. Capt. Hornsby, wounded. Ammunition in enemy's very heavy rain.	
" 24.9.15	Trenches very muddy. Our Artillery firing on the offensive. Cutting enemy's wire. Very little reply. Only a few shrapnel shell.	
" 25.9.15	Heavy rain all day. Our Artillery firing all day on German line & trenches. Very little reply.	
" 26.9.15	German Shelled Gun position at BIENVILLERS with shell of about 6" calibre. Between 30 and 40 shell sent over very rapidly. Some in Saturn trench. A great number failed to burst.	
27.9.15	Relieved in trenches by 12th Rifle Brigade. March back to billets at HUMBERCAMP	
28.9.15	Cleaning Billet	
29.9.15	600 men digging on Corps Line defences at SOUASTRE.	
30.9.15	300 men digging on Village defences at HUMBERCAMP	R.T. 10th L"Col Comm'd by Bedford Regt

(73989) W4141—463. 400,000. 9/14. H.&J.Ltd. Forms/C. 2118/10.

112th Inf.Bde.
37th Div.

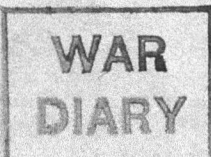

6th BATTN. THE BEDFORDSHIRE REGIMENT.

O C T O B E R

1 9 1 5

WAR DIARY

6/5/13 Bedfordshire Regt.

INTELLIGENCE SUMMARY.

Army Form C. 2118.

(Erase heading not required.)

Instructions regarding War Diaries and Intelligence Summaries are contained in F. S. Regs., Part II. and the Staff Manual respectively. Title pages will be prepared in manuscript.

Place	Hour, Date	Summary of Events and Information	Remarks and references to Appendices
HUMBERCAMP	1-10-15	In Billets - men employed digging defences round village.	
Do	2-10-15	As above.	
Do	3-10-15	} In Billets. Coy parades & working parties employed making wire entanglements round village defence line -	
	4-10-15		
	5-10-15		
Do	6-10-15	Battalion Route March. Very windy - cold & wet -	
Do	7-10-15	600 men employed digging on Corps line at Sovrast -	
Do	8-10-15	Men employed making wire entanglements round village defences.	
BIENVILLERS	9-10-15	Relieved 1st Bn Rifle Brigade in Billets at BIENVILLERS.	
	10-10-15	Working parties out all day & all night working on front-line trenches at HANNESCAMPS -	
	11-10-15	} As above.	
	12-10-15		
	13-10-15		
	14-10-15	As above. 2/Lt Aylwin wounded in HANNESCAMPS. Also Pte Clayton & Baker.	
HANNESCAMPS -	15-10-15	Relieved 10th L.N. Lancs Regt in trenches.	
	16-10-15	Artillery inactive on both sides. Weather damp & misty -	
	17-10-15	Enemy's artillery active on our front line. Fine weather - strong wind.	
	18-10-15	Our artillery active - L/Cpl Walk green on patrol from 4 a.m. to 6 p.m. & observed closed trenches in front of our line -	
	19-10-15	Germans fired minnenwerfers on right of our line - Germans artillery active on our trenches - Captain Blake - L/Cpl Nobbs, P. Smith wounded by shell burst in trenches. Pte Dean, Pte Smith	

WAR DIARY 6th (S) Bn Bedfordshire Regt
INTELLIGENCE SUMMARY.
(Erase heading not required.)

Instructions regarding War Diaries and Intelligence Summaries are contained in F. S. Regs., Part II. and the Staff Manual respectively. Title pages will be prepared in manuscript.

Hour, Date, Place	Summary of Events and Information	Remarks and references to Appendices
HANNESCAMPS. 19-10-15 (cont)	1st Columbine with 10 Bombers & scouts on patrol from 5:30 p.m. to 8:45 p.m. Pte Sahan killed while on this patrol.	
20-10-15	German artillery inactive - weather cold & misty	
BIENVILLERS. 21-10-15	Relieved in trenches by 13th Rifle Brigade - Took over new billets from 7th Leicester - Billets very good.	
22-10-15	Our artillery active but little reply from Germans.	
23-10-15	Parties digging by night.	
24-10-15	Working parties by day - Bombers practise - Pte Grantham & Townsend slightly wounded during practise by fay & injury. Coy parades.	
25-10-15 26-10-15 27-10-15 } In billets. Working parties by day & night.		
28-10-15 SAINT AMAND.	Relieved at BIENVILLERS by 11th R. Warwick Regt & went into billets at SAINT AMAND.	
29-10-15	Cleaning billets.	
30-10-15	Coy Parades	
31-10-15	600 men digging on Corps line at SOUASTRE.	Major for 1st Line [?] Major for 1st Support Line

R.W. Hylden (?)
Lt Col
Comdg 6 (S) Bn Beds Regt
(contd)

112th Inf.Bde.
37th Div.

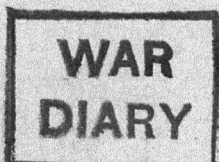

6th BATTN. THE BEDFORDSHIRE REGIMENT.

NOVEMBER

1915

WAR DIARY
or
INTELLIGENCE SUMMARY.

(Erase heading not required.)

Hour, Date, Place	Summary of Events and Information	Remarks and references to Appendices
1st November SAINT AMAND	Wet day - No working parties out	
2nd BIENVILLERS	Relieved at ST AMAND by 13th K.R.R. Marched to BIENVILLERS and relieved the 13th R.B. Weather very wet	
3rd "	Our Artillery active - Working parties from Batt.n employed on front line & communication trenches	
4th "	Enemy put a few shells into BIENVILLERS - no damage done - Working parties out as yesterday	
5th "	Working parties out as on previous day. Artillery active on both sides - Weather foggy.	
6th "	Working parties out as on previous day. B Coy. Front Line manning subsidiary line.	

INTELLIGENCE SUMMARY.

(Erase heading not required.)

Hour, Date, Place	Summary of Events and Information	Remarks and references to Appendices
Nov. 7th BIENVILLERS	Church Parade - lea the friars ...	
" 8th HANNES CAMP	Relieved 10th L.N. Lancs in trenches ... Trenches very hot & muddy.	
	H.Q. moved to HANNES CAMP. ...	
" 9th "	Heavy rain in the evening. Trenches very bad.	
" 10th "	Heavy rain all day. Trenches 89-90. to true enemy in water & mud. Regt. Lt. Col. Kitchener killed and Capt. Jackson slightly wounded by a shell.	
" 11th "	Fine morning - Very Cold. Men are employed cleaning & repairing trenches. Many Kitchener Bombs & Bangers fallen in?... Lieut Dare accidentally wounded by one of our men who mistook him for a German when he was returning from patrol ...	

INTELLIGENCE SUMMARY.

(Erase heading not required.)

Instructions regarding War Diaries and Intelligence Summaries are contained in F.S. Regs., Part II. and the Staff Manual respectively. Title pages will be prepared in manuscript.

Hour, Date, Place	Summary of Events and Information	Remarks and references to Appendices
12th Nov. HANNES CAMP.	Very hot night - Enemy firing a few small shell over Renekes 51 - 58.	
13th "	Much Colder - More rain in the night - Reneke still very hot - Many —	
14th "	Fine day - Relieved by 13th R.B. Marched back to HUMBERCAMP. Very cold. Hard frost	
15th HUMBERCAMP.	Fine day - 6 slight cases of Kenekes J. Kenek. first chugging. Last 6 days in very hot Reneke. Men taken Ambulance. First bite quite easily. Socks. Two sent out?) Reneke to be Ariès. Men's feet rubbed. A Co. went to Pas on refreshment. About 2 inches of snow fell during the night.	
16th "	Men went to Pas. to bathe.	
17th "	Fine day. Battn digging in 110th Brigade Area.	

INTELLIGENCE SUMMARY

(Erase heading not required.)

Instructions regarding War Diaries and Intelligence Summaries are contained in F.S. Regns., Part II. and the Staff Manual respectively. Title pages will be prepared in manuscript.

Hour, Date, Place	Summary of Events and Information	Remarks and references to Appendices
18th November	Hard frost in night. Very cold. Projects slightly however digging in 110th B?" area. Our heavy guns shelled Monchy.	
19th "	Batt'n digging in 110th B3" area. Our heavy guns firing on German.	
20th "	Very cold.	
21st "	Lieut Dan Severty Kennard blown out with working party in 110th B3" area & bullet in abdomen.	
22nd " HUBERCAMP?	Lieut Dan. Aird and Lan buried at HENU. near Pas.-en-Artois. – Company in trenches in line. Cutting with rifle attachment.	
23rd "	Army Commander inspected Bombers. Batt'n digging in 110th B3" Area	
24th "	Batt'n route march. 350 men digging.	

INTELLIGENCE SUMMARY.

(Erase heading not required.)

Instructions regarding War Diaries and Intelligence Summaries are contained in F.S.Regs., Part II. and the Staff Manual respectively. Title pages will be prepared in manuscript.

Hour, Date, Place	Summary of Events and Information	Remarks and references to Appendices
Nov 25th HUNBERCAMP.	A Coy returned from Pas.	
26th BIENVILLERS	Relieve 13th RB at BIENVILLERS. Very cold. Hard frost.	
27th "	Fine. Hard frost. Digging parties out.	
28th "	Hard frost. Men attacking Devine Service	
29th "	Thawing & Snow Storm. Relieved 10.N Lancs in trenches at HANNESCAMP. Very wet night	
30th HANNESCAMP.	Front trench trenches 51-M. Trench 59, 64 in a very bad state - water - mud knee deep. Sides of trenches continuously falling in owing to the sudden thaw. Communication trench below 57-57. dug in stages [?]. 2 large shells 6"&8" fire into HANNESCAMP but no damage done. Our artillery fairly active.	Ref. Plan right. See to 37. Down R-t-10th L"Coy by Bucks Regt 2/12/15

112th Inf.Bde.
37th Div.

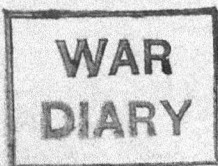

6th BATTN. THE BEDFORDSHIRE REGIMENT.

D E C E M B E R

1 9 1 5

6th Service Batt. Bedfordshire Regt.

WAR DIARY
or
INTELLIGENCE SUMMARY.
(Erase heading not required.)

Army Form C. 2118.

Hour, Date, Place	Summary of Events and Information	Remarks and references to Appendices
9th Dec. HUMBERCAMP.	In Brigade Reserve.	
10th–11th Dec. do.	Hot days. Batt. furnished working parties of 350 men for front line. 2/Lt. A Jessop joined on the 11th.	
12th Dec. do.	Muset Olden our Snow Shoes. 2/Lt. B.N. Colchester joined.	
13th to 15th Dec. do.	Order one foot at night. Furnished working parties for trenches on 15th.	
16th Dec. do.	Batt. did route march.	
17th–19th do.	Batt. digging on the 18th. Instructional Parades. Training 7 Grenadiers & Machine gun attachments. 2/Lt. R.F.G. Denning joined on the 19th.	
20th Dec. do.	Relieved 13th Batt. Rifle Brigade at BIENVILLERS. pro Batchelor Killed.	
21st–22nd BIENVILLERS.	Furnished working parties for front line trenches.	
23rd Dec. do.	Our Artillery bombarded German 9pdr. fertile.	
24th Dec. do.	Very wet night.	
25th Dec. do.	A little shelling in the morning. Otherwise very quiet day. Rained all day.	

6th Batt. Bedfordshire Regt

WAR DIARY
or
INTELLIGENCE SUMMARY.

(Erase heading not required.)

Army Form C. 2118.

Instructions regarding War Diaries and Intelligence Summaries are contained in F.S. Regs., Part II and the Staff Manual respectively. Title pages will be prepared in manuscript.

Hour, Date, Place		Summary of Events and Information	Remarks and references to Appendices
26th Dec.	BIENVILLERS	Hot day. Retired 10th N Lancs in the trenches	
27th Dec.	HANNESCAMP	German Shells hostring partie coming from BIENVILLERS - HANNESCAMP at 10 Shelled L/Corp Curry, L/Corp Hall and Pte Waters wounded. Very hot & our Communication trenches impassable	
28th Dec.	do.	Fine day. Germans shelled all our working parties coming up from BIENVILLERS. Shelled HANNESCAMP between 2 & 3 pm. 6 German aeroplanes came over on line, 4 of which got through and burst in direction of Souastre. 2 have turned back by our aircraft.	
29th Dec.	do.	German Artillery active. First line trenches are shelled from left to right. HANNESCAMP shelled at intervals during the day, but no material damage done. Our Artillery replies with some vigour. Aircraft on both sides active.	

6th Batt. Berkshire Regt

Army Form C. 2118.

WAR DIARY
or
INTELLIGENCE SUMMARY.
(Erase heading not required.)

Instructions regarding War Diaries and Intelligence Summaries are contained in F.S. Regs., Part II. and the Staff Manual respectively. Title pages will be prepared in manuscript.

Hour, Date, Place	Summary of Events and Information	Remarks and references to Appendices
30th Dec. HANNESCAMP.	Foggy morning. Low artillery activity.	
31st Dec. do.	2. Communication trenches have passed to tap in line. 48th Division on our right, heavily bombarded the German position between 12 and 2. German Sent 11 Shells into HANNESCAMP. No damage done. Rain in the afternoon. Short burst of rapid machine gun fire opened by both sides at midnight. Much rain in German lines. Stoke Mortars firing - 2 Minenwerfer Shells of largest calibre sent over at 12.10 a.m.	P.T. 10th Lieut. Col Commdg 6/ Berks Regt

December

6th Service Batt. The Bedfordshire Regt.

Army Form C. 2118.

WAR DIARY
or
INTELLIGENCE SUMMARY.
(Erase heading not required.)

Instructions regarding War Diaries and Intelligence Summaries are contained in F. S. Regs., Part II. and the Staff Manual respectively. Title pages will be prepared in manuscript.

Hour, Date, Place	Summary of Events and Information	Remarks and references to Appendices
1st December. HANNESCAMP.	Battalion in the trenches. Trenches very bad but quiet in trench.	Trench map. Sheet 57 D N.E. 1 & 2 (Part of) Scale 1:10000, Squares E. 11c, 17a, 16D, 21B
2nd Dec. do	Relieved in trenches by 10th Bn N Lancs. Regt. Marched back to BIENVILLERS in Support. Corpl Leete wounded.	
3rd Dec. BIENVILLERS	In Support Battn furnished working parties 2nd Lt C. Pigsam joined.	
4th Dec. do	Our Artillery shelled Germans in the morning. Enemy retaliated and sent about 100 shells into BIENVILLERS. Numerous small howitzer shells failing to explode - Private Walker & Oakley wounded. Subsequently died - Pts Hearst & Lancaster also wounded.	
5th Dec. do	Relieved by 10th N Lancs Regt. Battn moved up to trenches at HANNESCAMP.	
6th Dec. HANNESCAMP	Our Artillery shelled the Germans. Reply feeble.	
7th Dec do	Germans sent a few small howitzer shells into the trenches. Artillery bombardment at 3.45, to which the German replied. Rained all the afternoon. Sergt White wounded.	
8th Dec. do	Enemy shelled trenches 58-58½ No damage done. Relieved by 13th Rifle Brigade. Marched back to HUMBERCAMP	

(73989) W4141—463. 400,000. 9/14. H.&J.Ltd. Forms/C. 2118/10.

112th Brigade.
37th Division.

1/6th BATTALION BEDFORD REGIMENT

JANUARY 1 9 1 6

6th Service Batt. The Bedfordshire Regiment.

Army Form C. 2118.

WAR DIARY
or
INTELLIGENCE SUMMARY.
(Erase heading not required.)

Instructions regarding War Diaries and Intelligence Summaries are contained in F.S. Regs., Part II. and the Staff Manual respectively. Title pages will be prepared in manuscript.

Hour, Date, Place	Summary of Events and Information	Remarks and references to Appendices
1st Jan. 1916. HANNESCAMP.	Enemy more active at 11 p.m. last night (New year's eve German time) much shouting, blowing of Steam Whistle and musketry fire. Relieved in trenches by 13th Batt. Rifle Brigade. Marched back to billets in HUMBERCAMP.	
2nd Jany HUMBERCAMP.	Rest day. No working parties.	
3rd "	100 men digging at HANNESCAMP.	
4th, 5th "	Usual working parties on front line.	
6th "	Demonstration at Brigade Bombing ground, St AMAND by Lieut. Barnes, instruction of Machine Gunners in Grenadiers.	
7th "	100 men digging front line – C° Barnes, instruction of Machine Gunners in Grenadiers.	
8th "	Usual working parties + parades.	
9th "	Battn. Stood to + marched out to POMMIER Road. Gas practice alarm – Battn. been clear of the village in 35 minutes.	
10–12th "	Usual working parties on front line – Remainder of Battn. instruction Parades. Two Companies went to Grenade School for attack practice.	
13th "	Relieved the 13th Rifle Brigade at BIENVILLERS.	
14th BIENVILLERS.	A good deal of aerial activity by our aircraft. 2/Lt W. CANN joined on posting to Battn.	

1st Service Batt. Bedfordshire Regt

WAR DIARY
or
INTELLIGENCE SUMMARY.
(Erase heading not required.)

Army Form C. 2118.

Instructions regarding War Diaries and Intelligence Summaries are contained in F.S. Regs., Part II and the Staff Manual respectively. Title pages will be prepared in manuscript.

Hour, Date, Place	Summary of Events and Information	Remarks and references to Appendices
January, 1916.		
15th Jan. BIENVILLERS.	Duel. Wet day. Very little artillery activity	
16th " "	Air craft active on both sides.	
17th " "	Wet day. Combined Machine guns 110th + 112th Brigades. Concentrated fire on MONCHY at 6.20 p.m. 26 guns. Enemy's reply very feeble.	
18th " "	Duel and Rat. Quiet all day.	
19th " "	Our artillery active all morning. Germans fired 8. 77mm Shells into BIENVILLERS. Nos. 14221. Pte J. HUTCHINSON, No 15340 Pte J. THOMPSON (June 25.1.16), No 10683 Pte K.S. GIRLING. No 17564 Pte G. CARRINGTON. No 13223 L/Corp A WHITE wounded. Retired. 10th L.N. Lancs Regt at HANNESCAMP.	
20th " HANNESCAMP	Fine day. German FOKKER Aeroplane came over + dropped 3 bombs on BIENVILLERS. No damage done Germans Shelled Batt" H.Q." at HANNESCAMP. with 11 & 77 m.m. Shells. No material damage done. Trench 64 Shelled. No 12143. Capt M. BRAND, No 13852 Pte A. PRIOR. No 12490 Pte C. GREENSLADE, No 13490 Pte C.R. MITCHELL. Wounded. No 12093. L/Corp R. TAYLOR wounded + missing believed Killed. Still out sniping.	

6th Service Batt. Bedfordshire Regt.

WAR DIARY or INTELLIGENCE SUMMARY.

Army Form C. 2118.

Hour, Date, Place	Summary of Events and Information	Remarks and references to Appendices
January 1916		
21st Jan. HANNESCAMP	Artillery active on b.k. Sides.	
22nd " "	Artillery active on b.k. Sides. Bombardment by 48th Div. on our right between 2.30 + 3.30 p.m. No 10627 L/Corp. W. LAVENDER Wounded. 9265 J.B. HEALING + K.L. MALLET Joined on posting to Batt. Germans fired 30, 5.9" Howitzer Shells near batteries S.E. of BIENVILLERS. One Shell hit mile faster template. No damage done. Our Artillery retaliated at 12.10 p.m. D. Coy Sent out Strong Patrol which came back on German Patrol.	
23rd "		
24th " "	Foggy day - Quiet	
25th " "	Artillery activity on b.k. Sides between 1+2. a.m. near FONQUEVILLERS. - At 11.30 A.M. a German aeroplane flew over our lines and passed by to S.W. No 13073 Pte T. BAKER Wounded, Relieved by 13th Rifle Brigade. Marched back to billets at HUMBERCAMP.	
26th " HUMBERCAMP	Men at rest. Cleaning kit ve	

WAR DIARY
or
INTELLIGENCE SUMMARY.
(Erase heading not required.)

Army Form C. 2118.

Instructions regarding War Diaries and Intelligence Summaries are contained in F.S. Regs., Part II. and the Staff Manual respectively. Title pages will be prepared in manuscript.

Hour, Date, Place	Summary of Events and Information	Remarks and references to Appendices
January 1916		
27th Jan. HUMBER CAMP	Kaiser's birthday. — Air Guide on our front. Gas alarm about 7.30 p.m. Turned out to later on.	
28th "	Another Gas alarm. — later.	
29th "	Foggy all day. — Route Marching Bantin + Saraera	
30th "	Foggy all day. — "H.Q. O." route march "	
31st "	Wet fog all day. *B & Two Companies (B & D) Went to Brigade Grenade School to Practise Grenade attack.	
"	Route Marching Bantin.	

R.T. 1/6th Lieut. O.C.
Coun. 1/6 Bedford Regt

(73989) W.4141—463. 400,000. 9/14. H.&J.Ltd. Forms/C. 2118/10.

112th Brigade.
37th Division.

1/6th BATTALION BEDFORD REGIMENT

FEBRUARY 1 9 1 6:

6th Service Batt" Bedfordshire Reg"

WAR DIARY
or
INTELLIGENCE SUMMARY.

Army Form C. 2118.

February 1916

Hour, Date, Place	Summary of Events and Information	Remarks and references to Appendices
1.2.16 HUMBERCAMP.	Batt" in Brigade reserve. 2. Coy's route marching, remainder digging on front line.	
2nd & 3rd "	2. Coy's digging on front line. Marched out at night.	
4th . 5th "	Men digging on front line. Warmer with rain.	
6th BIENVILLERS	Relieve 13th Rifle Brigade at BIENVILLERS.	
7th to 9th "	Men employed digging on front line.	
10th HANNESCAMP.	Relieve N. Lancs Reg" in the trenches.	
11th "	Pte A. NORMAN slightly known by a shell.	
12th "	Following Casualties from Shell fire :- Lieut HITCH, 2/Lt MALLETT, Corp" HOLT, Ptes SUTHERLAND & COULDRIDGE. All wounded.	
13th "	Relieve in trenches by 6th Gloucester Reg" Marched back to St AMAND.	
14th. 15th St AMAND.	Battalion at rest.	
16th Trenches.	Relieve 9th Leicester Reg" in new sector of trenches near BIENVILLERS.	

6th Battn. Bedfordshire Regt.

WAR DIARY
or
INTELLIGENCE SUMMARY.

(Erase heading not required.)

Army Form C. 2118.

Instructions regarding War Diaries and Intelligence
Summaries are contained in F. S. Regs., Part II
and the Staff Manual respectively. Title pages
will be prepared in manuscript.

Hour, Date, Place 1916	Summary of Events and Information	Remarks and references to Appendices
February 17th Trenches.	Enemy shelled our Communication trench with 77 m.m. Shells – Pte BARTON known. (died 20.2.16)	
18th "	Hot day – quiet on our sector – Heavy bombardment by enemy on our trenches in front of FONQUEVILLERS.	
19th "	Hot day. Pte MERRIMAN Killed. Shot through the heart. Sergt SPRIGGS " " " " Zeppelin & 3 Aeroplanes came over about 11 p.m. Dropped 2 bombs near our H.Q. No damage done. Heavy bombardment S. of HEBUTERNE at 7 p.m.	
20th "	Fine day - Air Craft on both sides active Communication Trench Shelled with 77 m.m. Shells. Have frost at night.	
21st "	About 50, 77 m.m. Shells fire near Battn. H.Q. 5 hrs 9 Leicester Regt. wounded & 2 Killed PTE WILDER J. wounded - shot through the hand. Very cold. Snowing all morning	
22nd "	Relieved by 9th Leicester Regt. March back to ST AMAND	

6th Batt. Bedford Regt.

WAR DIARY
or
INTELLIGENCE SUMMARY.
(Erase heading not required.)

Army Form C. 2118.

Instructions regarding War Diaries and Intelligence Summaries are contained in F.S. Regs., Part II and the Staff Manual respectively. Title pages will be prepared in manuscript.

Hour, Date, Place 1916	Summary of Events and Information	Remarks and references to Appendices
February		
23rd 24th ST AMAND	Snowing all day, hard frost at night. About 500 men hutting, digging.	
25th "	Snowing all day	
26th-29th "	Thaw set in with rain. Been digging in front line every day.	

R. T. 10th L. Col
Commdg 6th Bedford Regt.

112th Brigade.
37th Division.

1/6th BATTALION

BEDFORD REGIMENT

MARCH 1916:

6/(?)B⁺ Bedfordshire Regt.

Army Form C. 2118.

WAR DIARY
or
INTELLIGENCE SUMMARY.
(Erase heading not required.)

Hour, Date, Place	Summary of Events and Information	Remarks and references to Appendices
1.3.16. SAINT AMAND	The Battalion took over new Billets at POMMIER.	
2ⁿᵈ, 3ʳᵈ & 4ᵗʰ POMMIER.	Battalion in Rest. Usual fat. 60 men working daily on front line.	
5ᵗʰ "	2ⁿᵈ Lt G.R.N. MORRISON posted to Bⁿ	Ref. Map 57D.N.E.Kn.6 1 & 2 (part 4)
6ᵗʰ "	Battalion moved to HANNESCAMPS & relieved 1/5 R Lancaster Regt in Trenches. Took over new line as per Column of Trench works. Put in Trenches.	1/10,000 E:17.A.3.6. – E.11.A.8.10.
7.3.16. HANNESCAMPS.	Quiet day. A certain number of trench mortar bombs & rifle Grenades were fired on the left of our lines by Ns.	
8.3.16. do.	Hostile Artillery inactive. Line extended on our right as per cor. of Remarks.	E:17.A.20 – E.11.A.8.10.
9 & 10ᵗʰ do.	Hostile Artillery Quiet. Enemy active with trench mortar bombs & rifle grenades. Good work done by Mt. snipers on both line days.	
11ᵗʰ do.	Hostile artillery shelled centre of line doing very little damage. Hostile trench mortar bombs active at Evening Stand to.	

6th (?) Staffordshire Regt.

WAR DIARY
or
INTELLIGENCE SUMMARY.
(Erase heading not required.)

Army Form C. 2118.

Hour, Date, Place	Summary of Events and Information	Remarks and references to Appendices
12.3.16. HANNESCAMPS.	Relieved in Trenches by 11th R. Warwick Regt. Headquarters proceeded to BIENVILLERS. A & C Coys. remained in HANNESCAMPS. B & D Coys proceeded to FONQUEVILLERS. 12044 Pte. Brand. W. Bullet wound in head. 13458 L/Cpl. Bull. G.F. Bullet wound in head.	
13.3.16. BIENVILLERS.	Battalion in Brigade Support. Day quiet. Weather fine and warm. 16481 Pte A. Sells. Bullet wound in head.	
14.3.16. Do.	300 men working on front line. Captain D'Alala rejoined. 4th R. PRICKETT arrived as a reinforcement. Day quiet.	
15.3.16. Do.	300 men working on front line. Aircraft on both sides active. Heavy shelling of HANNESCAMPS and BIENVILLIERS.	
16.3.16. Do.	Working parties to covered. Continued activity of hostile artillery. Exhibition of Flammenwurfen at LA CAUCHIE.	
17.3.16. Do.	Day quiet. Working parties to covered. Trenches traced. By Army Commander.	

6 (?) A: Bedfordshire Regt.

WAR DIARY
or
INTELLIGENCE SUMMARY.
(Erase heading not required.)

Army Form C. 2118.

Hour, Date, Place	Summary of Events and Information	Remarks and references to Appendices
18. 3. 16. NIENVILLIERS.	Working parties to counts. Day quiet. Heavy Artillery Bombardment on night of 18/19th on our right from 2 am to 3 am.	
19. 3. 16. -do-	Aerial activity on both sides. Relieved by 2nd Bn R. Irish Regt. Battalion moved to our Billets at HUMBERCAMPS. Trenches taken over by Royal Irish Fusiliers.	
HUMBERCAMPS. 20. 21st & 22nd	Battalion given 3 days complete rest on coming out of the trenches after a tour of seven days then employed cleaning up.	
23rd HUMBERCAMPS.	500 men digging on Corps line.	
24th -do-	Section & Platoon training started. Coy fatigues snow—	
25th -do-	do	

6/1/At Bedfordshire Regt.

WAR DIARY
or
INTELLIGENCE SUMMARY.
(Erase heading not required.)

Army Form C. 2118.

Hour, Date, Place	Summary of Events and Information	Remarks and references to Appendices
26.3.16. HUMBERCAMPS.	250 men working on Corps Line. Church Parade. Last day "A" Coy. A draft of 30 men arrived from 3rd. Entrenching Bn.	
27.3.16. -do-	250 men working on Corps Line. Remainder of Bn. Training. 2nd Lieut. W.H.B. SHERINGTON posted to "B" Coy.	
28.3.16. -do-	Bn. in training. Corps Commander visited Bn. H.Q.	
29.3.16. -do-	500 men working on Corps Line. Bn. inspected in billets by C in C. Swords in afternoon.	
30.3.16.	Training continued.	
31.3.16.	400 men on Corps. 2 bombs dropped on HUMBERCAMPS by hostile aeroplane. 12073 Pte. Carter H. slight shrapnel wound in head.	

R.W. Orpen. Major
Comdg 6th (M.S.) Bedfordshire Regt.

112th Brigade.
37th Division.

1/6th BATTALION BEDFORD REGIMENT

APRIL 1916

6th (S) B. Staffordshire Regt.

WAR DIARY
or
INTELLIGENCE SUMMARY.

XXXVII

Army Form C. 2118.

Hour, Date, Place	Summary of Events and Information	Remarks and references to Appendices
HUMBERCAMPS -		
1.4.16.	400 men working on Corps Line - Remainder training. 2/Lt. S.W.A. Peach proceeded to base as Instructor.	
2.4.16.	2/Lt. S.A.S. Child with draft of 30 men arrived.	
3+4-4-16.	400 men working on Corps Line	
5.4.16.	do	
6.4.16.	do - 2 Lt. J.M. Hewson posted to Btn. do - No. Sergt. W.S. FRANKLIN accidentally injured in head by bomb.	
7+8-4-16.	Took a turn in Corps Line -	
9-4-16.	Batt. relieved by 8th Leicester Regt. Proceeded to rest billets by route march to SUS-ST-LEGER.	
SUS-ST-LEGER.		
10-16-4-16.	520 men employed daily breaking kind Co - Remainder of Batt's Training -	

6th (OSB) = Bedfordshire Regt.

WAR DIARY
or
INTELLIGENCE SUMMARY.

Army Form C. 2118.

Hour, Date, Place	Summary of Events and Information	Remarks and references to Appendices
SUS - ST - LEGER. 17 - 20/4 - 16.	Batt. in training. - Water bad. -	
21. 4. 16.	Batt. inspected by Brigadier. Lieut W.M. WACE rejoined.	
23 - 4 - 16.	2nd Lieut R.E. CARLES - 2nd LIEUT. O.E. HODSON & 2nd Lt G. PEEL arrived as reinforcements.	
24/30/ 4 - 16.	Batt. employed finding 250 men daily hurdle making. Remainder of Batt.s training.	

R.M.M.Y........ Major ?/o
6th Bedfordshire Regt.

2/5/16.

112th Brigade.
37th Division.

1/6th BATTALION BEDFORD REGIMENT

M A Y   1 9 1 6

On His Majesty's Service.

D.A.G.
G.H.Q.
3rd Echelon
Base

War Diary of 6'S. Bn Bedfordshire Regt. Period 1st to 31st May.

B.

Absor in it
Neah

6 Bedfords
37/112
Vol 10

37

Army Form C. 2118.

WAR DIARY
or
INTELLIGENCE SUMMARY.
(Erase heading not required.)

Instructions regarding War Diaries and Intelligence Summaries are contained in F.S. Regs., Part II and the Staff Manual respectively. Title pages will be prepared in manuscript.

109

Hour, Date, Place	Summary of Events and Information	Remarks and references to Appendices
May 1st	Batt? retired from SUS — ST LEGER to BIENVILLERS.	
" 2	NIL	
" 3	Took over trenches 72 — 92 from 13/K.R.R.C. Bt. Maj. F.H. Edwards arrived & assumed command. Intense hostile bombardment followed by raid at 3am (66 casualties & 8 missing)	
" 4	NIL	
" 5	NIL	
" 6	NIL	
" 7	Relieved by 10th L.N. Lane. R.	
" 8	Working parties	
" 9	Ditto.	
" 10		

(73989) W4141—463. 400,000. 9/14. H.&J.Ltd. Forms/C. 2118/10.

Army Form C. 2118.

WAR DIARY
or
INTELLIGENCE SUMMARY.
(Erase heading not required.)

Instructions regarding War Diaries and Intelligence Summaries are contained in F. S. Regs., Part II. and the Staff Manual respectively. Title pages will be prepared in manuscript.

Hour, Date, Place	Summary of Events and Information	Remarks and references to Appendices
May 11 – 13 inclusive	Working parties (Bn H.Q. & 4 coys arrived on 12th)	
" 14	Batt'n moved to BAILLEULMONT (in relief of 9/R.F.)	
" 15 – 23 incl.	Working parties & training	
" 24	Seven (7) officers arrived from 9/Buff R.	
	" " " 8/Buff R.	
	54 men	
	8/ Retrenching Batt'n	
" 25	Training parties	
" 26	Moved to trenches 76 – 95	
" 27 }		
" 28 }	Quiet	
" 29 }		
" 30	Artillery (German) rather active on both sides. (1 killed 1 wounded)	

L.F. Edwards Lt-Col.
Comdg 6/Buff R.

112th Brigade.
37th Division.

Went with 112th Brigade to 34th Division
5th July 1916 - rejoined 37th Division
21st August 1 9 1 6

1/6th BATTALION BEDFORD REGIMENT

J U N E 1 9 1 6

6th Bedfords 27/112
June

Army Form C. 2118.
Vol II

XXXVII

WAR DIARY
or
INTELLIGENCE SUMMARY.
(Erase heading not required.)

Instructions regarding War Diaries and Intelligence Summaries are contained in F.S. Regs., Part II and the Staff Manual respectively. Title pages will be prepared in manuscript.

Hour, Date, Place	Summary of Events and Information	Remarks and references to Appendices
June 1st – 6th	In support at BIENVILLERS.	
" 6th	Moved to BAILLEULMONT.	
" 6th – 18th	BAILLEULMONT.	
" 14th	{ 1 Officer + 53 O.R. to 3rd Army Hd. Qrs.	
	8 O.R. to 37 C.C.S.	
" 16th	28 N.C.O's & men to AUXI-LE-CHATEAU	
" 18th to 24th	Moved to trenches opposite BIENVILLERS.	
" 24th	Moved out of trenches to BIENVILLERS.	
" 25th	{ 2. (O.R.) Killed	
	3. (O.R.) Died of Wounds.	
	16. (O.R.) Wounded	
" 26th & 27th	BIENVILLERS.	
	" 4 (O.R.) Wounded.	
" 28th & 29th	2 Coy. to support of 11th R. War. Regt. at HANNESCAMPS.	
" 30th	1. (O.R.) Killed	
	2. (O.R.) Wounded.	

110.

F. M. Edwards. Major.
Commdg. 6th Rg. Bn Bedfordshire Regt.

112th Brigade.
37th Division.
34th Division from 5th July.

Transferred with 112th Brigade from
37th to 34th Division 5th July 1916.

1/6th BATTALION

BEDFORDSHIRE REGIMENT

JULY 1916

6th Bn Bedford Regt.

Army Form C. 2118.

WAR DIARY
or
INTELLIGENCE SUMMARY.
(Erase heading not required.)

Instructions regarding War Diaries and Intelligence Summaries are contained in F.S. Regs., Part II and the Staff Manual respectively. Title pages will be prepared in manuscript.

Hour, Date, Place	Summary of Events and Information	Remarks and references to Appendices
July 1st BIENVILLERS	Battn in support (in Little)	
2nd	Battn moved from BIENVILLERS to HALLOY.	
3rd	AT HALLOY	
4th		
5th		
6th	Battn moved to MILLENCOURT by Lorries.	
7th	" USNA-TARA Line E of ALBERT	
8th	The last two Sundays at night –	
	Made in rear of 102nd attack	
	forming a defensive flank.	
	From CONTALMAISON. (Casualties - 4R + 14 w)	
	Same Position as 8th. (Casualties 14R + 1 missing. 5 OR + 70 wounded).	
9th	Same position as 9th. (Casualties 6R, 4 missing, 40 wounded)	
10th	Moved to support trench (1st HELIGOLAND)	
11th	Batt relieved in HELIGOLAND & found working party. (Casualties 2R. 1 missing, 7 w)	
12th	HELIGOLAND (1R + 22 w)	

S.?.Murray Capt.
Cmdg 6th Bn

6th Bn. Bedford Regt

Army Form C. 2118.

WAR DIARY
or
INTELLIGENCE SUMMARY.
(Erase heading not required.)

Instructions regarding War Diaries and Intelligence Summaries are contained in F.S. Regs., Part II. and the Staff Manual respectively. Title pages will be prepared in manuscript.

Hour, Date, Place	Summary of Events and Information	Remarks and references to Appendices
July 13.	Moved to USNA - TARA line.	
" 15.	Attack on POZIERES by 112th Bde from Pencho S of CONTALMAISON. Bn. held up by hostile machine gun. Satisfactions about 100x from its trench & dug in. Casualties {2 offrs K. {25 men K.} {9 offrs w. {174 OR W.} 32 B2 R.	
" 16.	Bn. moved to ALBERT	
" 18.	" BRESLE	
" 19-18	" LA HOUSSOYE	
" 20.		
" 21.	Batch of 120 arrived.	
" 22.	Bn. moved to BEHENCOURT.	
" 23/24	Draft of 26 arrived.	
" 25.	" 90 "	
" 30.	Bn. marched to BRESLE	
" 31.	" BECOURT WOOD 2500x E of ALBERT.	

J. Armond Lt Col
ComOff 6/Bed R

112th Brigade.
34th Division till 22nd August
rejoined 37th Division 22nd August 1916

1/6th BATTALION

BEDFORDSHIRE REGIMENT

AUGUST 1 9 1 6

Report on attack 9th August 1916 attached.

Army Form C. 2118.

WAR DIARY
or
INTELLIGENCE SUMMARY.
(Erase heading not required.)

Instructions regarding War Diaries and Intelligence Summaries are contained in F. S. Regs., Part II. and the Staff Manual respectively. Title pages will be prepared in manuscript.

Hour, Date, Place	Summary of Events and Information	Remarks and references to Appendices
Aug 1st 1916	Batt at BÉCOURT WOOD.	
" 3rd "	11 Officers arrived	
" 5th "	To trenches at BOTTOM WOOD west of FRICOURT	
" "	1 Offr. 16 O.R. wounded on bombing party.	
6a. Fri	2 O.R. Bar. 2 Lt. BAZENTIN-LE-PETIT (1 O.R. wounded)	
" 7 "	8 O.R. killed. 1 Offr & 24 O.R. wounded.	
" 8 "	1 O.R. killed. 1 Offr. & 13 O.R. wounded. Intermediate	
" "	line attacked at 9.30 am.	
" 9 "	1 Offr & 8 O.R. killed. 25 O.R. missing. 2 Offrs & 49 O.R. wounded.	
" 10 "	1 Offr & 1 O.R. killed. 12 O.R. wounded. Batt 2nd to support	
" "	Nineteen billets (BAZENTIN-LE-PETIT WOOD)	
" "	MAMETZ WOOD.	
" 11 "	1 Offr & 7 O.R. wounded at R.E.	
" 13 "	Batt. to BÉCOURT WOOD. 1 O.R. killed 3 O.R. wounded	
" 15 "		
" 16 "	Batt: marched to BAZENCOURT	
" 17 "	Draft of 5 Offrs & 288 new arrivals.	

(73989) W.4141—463. 400,000. 9/14. H.&J.Ltd. Forms/C. 2118/10.

Army Form C. 2118.

WAR DIARY
or
INTELLIGENCE SUMMARY.
(Erase heading not required.)

Instructions regarding War Diaries and Intelligence Summaries are contained in F.S. Regs., Part II. and the Staff Manual respectively. Title pages will be prepared in manuscript.

Hour, Date, Place	Summary of Events and Information	Remarks and references to Appendices
July 18. 1916	Entrained at TRECHENCOURT for LONGPRÉ & marched to AIRAINES	
" 20	Marched from LONGPRÉ AIRAINES to LONGPRÉ & entrained to ESTAIRES	
" 21	Arrived at BAILLEUL & marched to ESTAIRES	
" 22	Entrained at LA GORGUE & detrained at CALONNE RICOURT & then marched to BRUAY. Rejoined 37 Div.	
" 24	Marched to MAZINGARBE. Tpt NOEUX LES MINES.	
" 25	To trenches in LOOS SALIENT (Bnto 14 Bde). Tpt. on loan to 40 DH.	
" 26	2 OR. Killed 6 OR wounded.	
" 27	1 OR wounded.	
" 29	Batt : to MAZINGARBE	
" 30		
" 31	At MAZINGARBE	

MESSAGES AND SIGNALS.

Army Form C. 2121

Prefix	Code	m.	Words	Charge	This message is on a/c of:	Recd. at	m.

Office of Origin and Service Instructions.

Sent
At .... m.
To ....
By ....

Service.
(Signature of "Franking Officer.")

Date ....
From ....
By ....

TO { 112th Bde

Sender's Number. | Day of Month. | In reply to Number. | A A A

At	9.15 am	a	heavy	artillery
barrage	was	opened	by	the
Germans	which	enfiladed	our	trenches
This	fire	became	from	the
direction	of	41G4	Patrols	at
9.30 am	Nos	1, 2, 3, & 4	*stated*	& the
the	trenches	No 5	It	Jessen
party	under	It	O.C. B	Coy
because	ordered	by	Elements	of
till	artillery fire	slackened	over	the
Nos 1 & 2	Patrols	got	held	up
ridge	but	were	rifle	line
by	M.G.	&	great	difficulty
No 3	Patrol	had	of	the
in	getting	out	officer	was
trench	&	the	soon as	he
rendered	unconscious	as	soon as	he

From
Place
Time

The above may be forwarded as now corrected.

(Z)

Censor. | Signature of Addressee or person authorised to telegraph in his name.

* This line should be erased if not required.

225,000. W 14042—M 44. H. W & V., Ld. 12/15.

@ Saunders

Army Form C. 2121.

...AND SIGNALS.

got	on	the	parapet.	This
patrol	appears	to	have	become
somewhat	disorganised	&	did	not
get	very	far	forward.	
No. 4	patrol	had	both	officer
&	Sergeant	killed.		
No. 5	patrol	suffered	most	casualties
losing	its	officer	&	2 Sergts.
Lt	Saunders	i/c No. 2	Patrol	says that
he	could	see	Germans	manning
the	trench.	His	impression	seems
to	be	that	there	are
at	least	2 M.G.s	between	the
Block	& S.ed	~~~~	road	through
S.ed	central.			
Lt	Jesson	who	was	asking

SIGNALS. — Army Form C. 2121.

For the C.T. at S 2c 8.4, could not get within bombing distance being of M.G. fire & rifle fire. Fire also appears to here come from the switch line & from a NE direction. Perhaps High Wood. The patrols found shell-holes sand-bagged in front of the intermediate line. My own impression is that the intermediate line is strongly held with M.G.s & rifle-men & has not been much damaged by our artillery fire. If a future attempt is made under a barrage, the

SIGNALS.

Army Form C. 2121.

No. of Message ....

Office of Origin and Service Instructions.

Words | Charge
Sent
At .... m.
To ....
By ....

This message is on a/c of:

4 Service.
(Signature of "Franking Officer.")

Recd. at .... m.
Date ....
From ....
By ....

TO {

Sender's Number.	Day of Month.	In reply to Number.	**A A A**

hostile artillery in the direction of HIGH WOOD must be Smothered if heavy casualties are to be avoided

J.H. Edwards Lt Col
Comdg 1/4 Beds R.

9/8/16.

From
Place
Time

The above may be forwarded as now corrected. (Z)
.... Censor.   Signature of Addressor or person authorised to telegraph in his name.
* This line should be erased if not required.
225,000. W 14042—M 44. H. W & V., Ld. 12/15.

No. 6

Operation orders by Lt. Col. Edwards
Commdg 6th Bedf R.

8.8.16

1. The capture of the enemy's intermediate line between S.2.d.9.5 + S.2.c.8.4 will be completed tonight by this battalion.

2. At 9.30 p.m. 3 patrols from A. Coy + 2 from B. Coy each consisting of 1 officer + 25 men will leave the present front line & occupy the enemy's intermediate. These patrols will be numbered from the right as 1, 2, 3, 4 + 5. Each will have a Lewis Gun.

3. No. 1 patrol will occupy the intermediate line 50ˣ N. of the block between S. E/Lan. R. + the enemy.
No. 2 patrol - half way between No 1. + the road running thro' S.2.d. central.
No. 3 patrol astride the road running thro' S.2.d. central.
No. 4. patrol about 100ˣ W. of the road thro S.2.d. central.
No. 5. patrol about 100ˣ E. of road running through S. 2. c. 8. 4.

4. An independent party of 16 men under 2/Lt Jesson will block the communication trench running N. to the Switch line from S.2.c.8.4. The method will depend upon the state of the trench, but the enemy must be kept 60ˣ from our block. A Lewis Gun will accompany this party.

5. As soon as a patrol occupies the intermediate line, it will fire one white Very Light at an angle of about 20° towards our present front line & send back an orderly to report at Report Centre.

6. O.C. A & B Coys will be responsible for conduct of operations E. & W. respectively of road running thro' S.2.d. central. They will send up the Pioneer Coy (2 platoons of which are allotted to each) to carry out the work of consolidation as soon as the intermediate line is occupied.

7. When the front line is vacated by A. & B. Coys it will be occupied by C. Coy & D. Coy will extend its line to occupy the trenches held by C. Coy.

8. O.C. C. Coy will make arrangements to carry forward bombs, tools, S.A.A. & Sandbags as required. He will also commence a communication trench from S.2.d.1.2. towards the enemy's line.

9. In the event of complete occupation of the intermediate line, the 46th Bde on our left will run a C.T. from S.2.c.8.4. to S.2.c.8.5 & the 8th E. Lan. R. will press toward our right & consolidate for 50ˣ N. of the block at S.2.d.8.5. 2/Lt Jesson will keep troops of the 46th Bde informed of his progress.

10. If any patrol is held up, it will be reinforced by its respective Coy +if necessary by O.C. C. Coy.

11. The 'report centre' will be at S.2.d.7.2. + will be manned by Signallers of A. Coy.

12. Battalion Hdqrs will remain as at present.

Copy. no. 1. O.C A.Coy   5 O.C. 8th E. Lan. R.
        2   " B.   6 112th Inf. Bde.
        3   " C.   7 Retd.
        4   " D.

Issued at 5.30 p.m   W.J. Cunningham
    by orderly   Lt +adjt.
                                      6th Bedf. R
8. 8. 16.

112th Brigade.
37th Division.

1/6th BATTALION BEDFORD REGIMENT

SEPTEMBER 1 9 1 6

Army Form C. 2118.

6. Beaufort

WAR DIARY
or
INTELLIGENCE SUMMARY.
(Erase heading not required.)

Instructions regarding War Diaries and Intelligence Summaries are contained in F.S. Regs., Part II. and the Staff Manual respectively. Title pages will be prepared in manuscript.

Hour, Date, Place	Summary of Events and Information	Remarks and references to Appendices
Sept. 1st 1916	Marched from HAZEBROUCK to NOEUX-LES-MINES	
" 2d "	" NOEUX-LES-MINES to DIÉVAL. Rec'd draft 20 O.R.	
" 3d "	Inspection by G.O.C. 37/ Div.	
" 2d - 18th	Batt'n remained at DIÉVAL.	
	Draft of 9 O.R. arrived.	
" 15th "	2 Offrs arrived as reinforcements.	
" 17th "	Moved from DIÉVAL to FOSSE 10 (SAINS-EN-GOHELLE) Rec'd 3 Offrs.	
" 18th "	To trenches in Sector ANGRES I R.N. Div'n	
" 19 "	Relieving ANSON BATT'N R.N. Div'n	
" 25th "	From trenches to BULLY-GRENAY	
" 30 "	BULLY-GRENAY.	

St Laurence Lt. Col.
Cmdg 6/Beauf R.

112th Brigade.
37th Division.

1/6th BATTALION BEDFORD REGIMENT

OCTOBER 1 9 1 6

WAR DIARY
or
INTELLIGENCE SUMMARY.
(Erase heading not required.)

Army Form C. 2118.

VOL 15

Hour, Date, Place	Summary of Events and Information	Remarks and references to Appendices
Nov 1st 1916	In trenches in ANGRES I	
" 6 "	4 O.R. wounded.	
" 7 "	Iron trenches to BOUVIGNY — BOYEFFLES. (FOSSE 10)	
" 8 "	1 O.R. wounded	
" 13 "	In trenches in ANGRES I	
" 15 "	Relieved by Canadians & marched to VERDREL	
" 16 "	Marched to LA COMPTE	
" 16 "	" TERNAS	
" 20 "	" REBREUVE.	
" 21 "	" LONGUEVILLETTE	
" 22 "	" SARTON	
" 23 "	" BEAUSSART (Nialo Thienues)	
" 25 "	" ARQUEVES	
" 27 "	" SARTON.	
" 31 "		

Sylvester Bent
Col
RM

150

112th Brigade.
37th Division.

1/6th BATTALION   BEDFORD REGIMENT

NOVEMBER 1 9 1 6

Army Form C. 2118.

WAR DIARY
or
INTELLIGENCE SUMMARY.
(Erase heading not required.)

Place	Date	Hour	Summary of Events and Information	Remarks and references to Appendices
SARTON	1st–11th		[Waiting for Formation of mentor for offensive operations.]	
	12th		Marched to LOUVENCOURT.	
	13th		" to BERTRANCOURT at 3pm.	
	13th		" " MAILLY – MAILLET at 7pm.	
	14th		" " " assembly in TOURNAI TRENCH near MAILLY-MAILLET at midday.	
	14th		At 2 am. marched forward to attack FRANKFORT TRENCH at midnight.	
	14th		Went forward to attack FRANKFORT TRENCH with rest of the 112th Bde. 4 officers killed.	
	15th		Attacked MUNICH TRENCH with rest of the 112th Bde. arriving at 6-30 am.	
	15th		Extricate near WAGGON ROAD	
	16th		WAGGON ROAD to MAILLY – MAILLET.	
	16th		Marched from WAGGON ROAD	
	17th		Marched to ENGLEBELMER.	
	17th		Left ENGLEBELMER at 8am for a cutting between HAMEL & BEAUCOURT.	
	18th		Remained in the cutting finding carrying parties for 111th & 113th Bdes	
	19th		To front line trenches between BEAUMONT HAMEL & BEAUCOURT	
	20th–21st			
	22nd		To MAILLY to Picardy in STATION ROAD (shelters)	
	22nd		4 100 men under Capt. Pegler associated to L.N. Lanc Regt in an attack on the	
	23rd		Enemy trenches at the Eastern end of MUNICH & FRANKFORT TRENCH TRIANGLE	

Army Form C. 2118.

WAR DIARY
or
INTELLIGENCE SUMMARY.
(Erase heading not required.)

Instructions regarding War Diaries and Intelligence Summaries are contained in F. S. Regs., Part II. and the Staff Manual respectively. Title pages will be prepared in manuscript.

Place	Date	Hour	Summary of Events and Information	Remarks and references to Appendices
	24 } 25 }		Remained in Quarry in STATION ROAD.	
	26		Marched to MAILLY-MAILLET at 7a.m.	
	27		Marched to ACHEUX WOOD	
	30		Marched to RUBEMPRE.	

L.H. Henderson Lt
Acting Adjt Bedf R.

112th Brigade.
37th Division.

1/6th BATTALION BEDFORD REGIMENT

DECEMBER 1 9 1 6

Army Form C. 2118.

6 Bedford Rgt

WAR DIARY
or
INTELLIGENCE SUMMARY.
(Erase heading not required.)

Instructions regarding War Diaries and Intelligence Summaries are contained in F. S. Regs., Part II. and the Staff Manual respectively. Title pages will be prepared in manuscript.

17a

Oct 1917

Hour, Date, Place	Summary of Events and Information	Remarks and references to Appendices
Dec 1st. 1916.	at RUDEMPRE	
5. "	2 Offrs arrived as reinforcements	
7. "	1 " " " "	
8. "	1 " " " "	
9. "	1 " " " "	
10. "	1 " " " "	
11. "	Draft of 154 O.R. arrived.	
13. "	Marched to BEUVAL	
14. "	" " BONNIÈRES	
15. "	" " NUNCQ.	
16. "	" " BOURS	
17. "	" " LIÈRES	
18. "	" " ST VENANT	
20. "	" " BETHUNE	
22. "	" " LA COUTURE	
28. "	Bde in trenches in FERME DU BOIS Sector	
	{ 1 Offr. arrived (Lt Lucas).	
30. "	4 O.R. wounded.	

J.S. Erneminger Lt Col
by J.S. Bent

37/112

Vol 8

War Diary
of
6th Bedfords.
January 1917.

Army Form C. 2118.

WAR DIARY
or
INTELLIGENCE SUMMARY.
(Erase heading not required.)

Instructions regarding War Diaries and Intelligence Summaries are contained in F.S. Regs., Part II and the Staff Manual respectively. Title pages will be prepared in manuscript.

Hour, Date, Place	Summary of Events and Information	Remarks and references to Appendices
1.1.1917	Battalion in the trenches at FERME du BOIS (S. of NEUVE CHAPELLE).	
2.1.1917	Lt. W.E. Ayloun awarded the Military Cross. Lt Col J M Edwards, Lt C Chauner & R S M. Headland mentioned in despatches	
3.1.'17	Batn to support trials at LE TOURET. Draft of 50 O.R. arrived as reinforcements.	
8.1.17	Four officers arrived as reinforcements.	
9.1.17	Batn to trenches in same Sector.	
10.1.17	Heavy bombardment of enemy trenches by our artillery & trench mortars. Four men wounded during the retaliation.	
11.1.17	50 O.R. arrived as reinforcements.	
15.1.'17	31 " Batn to LE TOURET.	
17.1.'17	1 officer arrived as reinforcement.	
21.1.'17	Batn to trenches in same sector. Weather very cold & frosty.	
22.1.17	38 O.R. arrived as reinforcements.	
23.1.17	2 Prisoners captured by our wiring party. D.S.M. abbots awarded	
24.1.17	3 officers arrived as reinforcements.	
	the D.C.M.	
28.1.17	Batn to LE TOURET.	
29.1.17	Batn relieved by 10th Yorks Lancs. Regt of the 63rd Inf. Bde & returned to the reserve brigade area at ZELOBES.	

W.Cunningham Lt & Adjt for Lt Col Commdg 6th IxnBedf. Regt

WAR DIARY

Vol 19

M L Stafford

Feby 1917

Army Form C. 2118.

WAR DIARY
or
INTELLIGENCE SUMMARY.
(Erase heading not required.)

Instructions regarding War Diaries and Intelligence Summaries are contained in F.S. Regs., Part II and the Staff Manual respectively. Title pages will be prepared in manuscript.

Hour, Date, Place	Summary of Events and Information	Remarks and references to Appendices
1. 2. 17.	Marched to ROBECQ	
3.	103 O.R. arrived as reinforcements.	
10.	Marched to NOEUX-LES-MINES	
11.	" " LES BREBIS.	
17.	Took the trenches LOOS (2 Offrs arrived)	
18.	2 killed 4 wounded.	
19.	1 " 2 "	
21.	1 " 1 "	
23.	To MAROC (in support)	
25.	11 O.R. arrived as reinforcements.	
26. 27. 28.	Took the trenches LOOS.	

J. H. Gunning Lt. Col.
B. Berthier

Army Form C. 2118.
37/12

1 Bedford Regt
Nov 20

WAR DIARY
or
INTELLIGENCE SUMMARY.
(Erase heading not required.)

Instructions regarding War Diaries and Intelligence Summaries are contained in F.S. Regs., Part II. and the Staff Manual respectively. Title pages will be prepared in manuscript.

Hour, Date, Place	Summary of Events and Information	Remarks and references to Appendices
1. 3.17. LOOS.	In trenches (O.R. + 5 C.S.)	
2.	L. Billets LES BREBIS (1R + 6 C.S.)	
3.	" BETHUNE	
4.	" ROBECQ	
5.	" LINGHESDELGUES	
6.	" FLECHIN	
6.	" MATHON	
9.	" ETREE - WAMIN	
10.	2/Lts Dickens & Smith arr. as reinf.	
15.	6 O.R. reinf.	
16.	2/Lt Liddle arrived	
23.		
31.	Batt'n training at ETREE - WAMIN	

SECRET.
Vol 21

War Diary for
April 1917

6th Bedfordshire Regt.

WAR DIARY
or
INTELLIGENCE SUMMARY.
(Erase heading not required.)

Army Form C. 2118.

Instructions regarding War Diaries and Intelligence Summaries are contained in F.S. Regs., Part II and the Staff Manual respectively. Title pages will be prepared in manuscript.

Hour, Date, Place	Summary of Events and Information	Remarks and references to Appendices
2.4.17 ETREE-WAMIN	Bn. drills. Fag parties. Bgde. Efficiency competition won by No. 3 Coy.	
5 —	Marched to HAUTEVILLE.	
7 —	" " WANQUETIN	
8 —	" " WARLUS	
9 —	" " ARRAS & new fighting equipment. Advanced to road running N. & S. thro' FEUCHY CHAPELLE & dug in.	
10 —	Captured LA FOLIE FERME & LA BERGERE in conjunction with attack of 111th Bde on MONCHY-LE-PREUX. Lt Shaw killed. Bn. extended on line LA BERGERE Cross-roads — GUEMAPPE. 2/Lts Bestall, Hedges, Latham, Rainham, Epiman wounded. Lt Thompson killed. Relieved at night & remained on the above line.	
11 —	Rejoined 12th Bde.	
12 —	Marched to lock bivouacs in TILLOY. Several men suffered from Epsom gas. Marched to ARRAS, thence by train to WANQUETIN. After daylight marched to WARLUS.	
14 —	Marched to GIVENCHY-LE-NOBLE-LATTRE.	
16 —	2/Lts ROSE, LOVE, FOSSETT & NOKES arrived.	
17 —	Lewis Gun carts finally given up.	
19 —	Marched to LATTRE - ST-QUENTIN.	
21 —	" " ST NICHOLAS & bivouaced.	
23 —	" " EFFIE TRENCH for attack on GREENLAND HILL Carried out at 4.25 am. Bn advanced to support the 63rd Bde. — & Berlin at 9.45 said between ROEUX & BAVRELLE. Finally dug in E. of said letter. Staffs, Parson, Nokes wounded Lts Buckle & Williams, Lt Molloy, Bestall killed.	
24 —		

WAR DIARY
or
INTELLIGENCE SUMMARY.
(Erase heading not required.)

Army Form C. 2118.

Hour, Date, Place	Summary of Events and Information	Remarks and references to Appendices
25.4.17	2Batt" Standards in trench of last day.	
26.	Do.	
27.	Do.	
28.	Batt" assembles for attack (at dawn) on GREENLAND HILL. Section almost gassed. Parties dug in close supp. and Suffolk farm. Suffered from CHEMICAL works when sup. of 2nd Batt. Gorm Rifles & the Line & a party missing after relief by Moors to BERLEN– held up. 6 MPRHS after relief & barricaded by attack. Lt. Rose Reached Court. Only 58 men actually came out of the attack. Lps. Williams & POSKETT killed. Lts Rather & Smith wounded. Lps Williams & Brown wounded.	

Lt. Col.
61 Bedf.

SECRET

Copy No........

OPERATION ORDERS
by Lieut Col F.A. Edwards
Commdg 6th "S"Bn Bedfordshire Regt.
7-4-17

Ref Maps
51.b. & 51.c.
(1/80,000)
Maps of ARRAS &
Trench Maps as
issued

1. **INFORMATION.** The enemy occupy MONCHY LE PREUX and have entrenchments between MONCHY LE PREUX and GUEMAPPE as well as defended posts on the CAMBRAI Road.

2. **INTENTION.** In the attack by the 37th Division on MONCHY LE PREUX the 6th Bedford Regt will seize the line N.12.c.9.2. - WINDMILL, N.12.b.4.1. inclusive and occupy the village of GUEMAPPE.

3. **POINT OF ASSEMBLY.** Until ordered to advance to the BROWN LINE the Battalion will assemble in the present BRITISH FRONT LINE Trenches between the CAMBRAI Road and ICELAND STREET.
    Front Line "C"Coy, Right - "B"Coy, Left.
    Second Line "A" "   " - "D" " "
Hd Qrs in IMPERIAL STREET (G.29.d.9.5.) or ST SAUVEUR defences line (G.29.d.4.4.)

4. **TOUCH WITH 3RD DIVISION.** On arrival at the BLUE LINE O.C. "C"Coy will send out a patrol to keep touch with Hd Qrs of the rearmost Battalion of the 3rd Division, as 6th Bedford Regt must be prepared to assist the 3rd Division in its attack on the BROWN LINE.

5. **ADVANCE TO BROWN LINE.** The advance to the BROWN LINE will be made in Artillery Formation; the centre of the Battalion will direct along the CAMBRAI ROAD.
"D" and "B" Companies will move North of the CAMBRAI ROAD. "C" and "A" Companies, South of the CAMBRAI RD.

6. **REFORMING OF THE BATTALION.** The Battalion will reform on arrival at Road running North and South through FEUCHY CHAPEL, half of "D" and "B"Companies remaining North of the CAMBRAI RD. and the remainder of the Battalion, South of it.

7. **ADVANCE TO OBJECTIVE.** The Battalion will subsequently advance on a frontage of 500 yards with its left 100 yards North of the CAMBRAI ROAD. Touch will be maintained with the 8th E.Lancs Regt on the left
10th L.N.Lancs Regt will be in support.
11th Roy.Warwick Regt will be in Brigade Reserve.
No forward move will take place until ordered by Battalion Hd Qrs.

8. **FORMATION FOR ATTACK ON OBJECTIVE.** The formation for attack will be four waves but O.C. Companies must use their own discretion as to points where Artillery Formation or Extended Order is most suitable.

9. **CYCLISTS.** The Cyclist Battalion (Less One Company) will protect our Right Flank and connect up with the VII Corps during the advance on MONCHY LE PREUX. It will also reinforce the detachment of "C"Company,6th Bedford Regt ordered to occupy GUEMAPPE after MONCHY LE PREUX has been cleared of the enemy.

10. TANKS. At Zero -5 minutes, the Tanks if employed, will move forward (Zero in this particular case being hour fixed for the advance of Infantry to attack the GREEN LINE) to the line - WOOD, O.8.central - WOOD in O.8.d. - ACHILLES COPSE, dealing with strong points en route. After the Infantry have established posts on this line, the Tanks will withdraw behind the CREST and remain in support of the posts.

11. FLARES. Flares will be lit on the GREEN LINE at Zero + 12 hours. They will be lit in addition when called for by aeroplanes i.e., A succession of A's on the Klaxon Horn. If no reply is received, the aeroplane will fire a white light indicating a call for flares.

12. POSITION OF B.H.Q. When the Battalion moves forward from the BROWN LINE B.H.Q. will be in FEUCHY CHAPEL REDOUBT and afterwards at GORRE FERME. Look outs will be posted by B.H.Q. near the CAMBRAI ROAD to stop runners with messages. B.H.Q. will be marked by a flag of Regimental Colours marked "B.H.Q."

M. Cunningham

Issued by Orderly
at   pm.

Lieutenant,
& Adjutant,
6th "S"Battn Bedfordshire Regiment

Copy No. 1. C.O.
"   " 2 Retained
"   " 3 O.C. "A" Coy
"   " 4 "   " "B" "
"   " 5 "   " "C" "
"   " 6 "   " "D" "
"   " 7 Signal Officer
"   " 8 Sniping Officer
"   " 9 112th Inf Bde (For Information)

SECRET

OPERATION ORDERS
by Lt. Col. F. A. Edwards
Commdg 6th Bedfordshire Regt.

Ref Maps
51.b & 51 c (1/40000)   8-4-17

1. The Battn will move off from present camp at 3.45 am tomorrow and proceed to EQUIPMENT DUMP West of ARRAS where fighting equipment will be picked up & a hot meal taken.

2. Order of march — Hd.Qrs - "C" - "D" - "A" - "B" Coys. Cookers - Mess Cart - Maltese Cart - Lewis Gun Limbers & Signal Limber will follow in rear of Battn. Remainder of transport will move under orders from Bde Transport Officer. The whole Battn will move as far as the dump where one days rations will be drawn by all ranks. Reinforcements will move back from this point to new Transport Lines in L.23.c under the orders of Maj. Mackenzie. The Carrying party of 100 men as already detailed will remain at the Equipment Dump when the Battn moves forward to the attack & will come under the orders of 2/Lt. Crauswick.

3. Blankets will be rolled in bundles of 10 & will be left with the packs & Great Coats. Valises will also be left at the Great coat & pack dump.

until called for by the Br. Hqrs.
1 man per toy as already detailed will be left behind at the Park Dump when the Batty moves off from its present camp.

4. Camping Ground to be left as clean as possible.

5. There will be tea at 2.45 a.m.

Mr. Cunningham
Lt & adjt
6th Batt R.

7 p.m. 7.4.17

6. Unless otherwise notified Reinforcements will remain behind when the Batt. moves from its present camp in the morning, and will move forward under the orders of Maj. Mackenzie.

Sgt's R.Bau
C.O 13.4.17

Diary of Events.
April 9th – 17th 1917.

9.4.17. Batt'n left WARLUS at 3.45 a.m & reached dump W. of Arras at 5.30 a.m.

9.30 a.m. moved from the dump to take up positions in front line.

1 p.m. 2 Coys in position on German front line N.15. of CAMBRAI, with 2 Coys in Support in O.B. line.

At 3 p.m. 2 Coys were on line DEVIL'S WOOD – H.31.A.

4 p.m. B'n moved to corner of OBSERVATION RIDGE N. of the CAMBRAI Rd.

6.15 p.m. B'n moved N. of CAMBRAI Rd & reached broad running N. & S. through FEUCHY CHAPEL, about

7.10 p.m. No further advance could be made owing to uncut wire. In there were position of Bedfords, Warwick, E.York, R.S. & Fusiliers, Gordons, & Essex. S.L.I. on this road, there was considerable congestion.

O.C. 6th Bedf'n withdrew Warwicks 150x W. of road, dug in, & asked other units to prolong line of the Bedfords on the road to the right, as there appeared to be no definite line beyond N.9.a.0.3. Posts were established in front of the road & during the night the 6th Bedf'n attempted to cut through the wire in the F.C. line. This was impossible.

10.4.17. At 2.30 a.m. orders were received from the 19th Bde to withdraw from the road & enable the artillery to cut the wire.

5.30 a.m. Artillery commenced to cut wire which did not enable Inf'y to attack before noon.

1 p.m. F.C. System was crossed by 6 Div Div'n & the whistle was waived & advance to the spur running S. between MONCHY + GUEMAPPE. The R. & R. reached the sunken lane N. of a S.E. Light railway N.a.4.4. Div'n.

the most advanced line the Bn. eve. reached S. of CAMBRAI road towing [enfilade] fire from both flanks had to be withdrawn about 300x where men the dug in. This line was well established at about 10 p.m. & covered by posts & patrols. Night was quiet - touch with some cyclists est. about M.17. central.

11.4.17. 4.50. a.m. orders recd for the Battn to move N. of the CAMBRAI Rd. & become Battn in Bde reserve. This entailed a move to a flank under machine gun fire which entailed a certain amount of loss. The Battn here became Battn in Bde reserve, but with portions of L.N.L., War. & K.L. with a Vickers gun of the 110th Bde M.G.C occupied lines in a frontage of about 300x. These lines ran // with the road to MONCHY from LA BERGERE the right of each resting on the CAMBRAI road between Hex 2do & the enclosure at H.17.d.7.4 & were about 120x apart. Touch with the cavalry was gained at road junction O.7.a.1.8. At this period, the Germans were recapping a line about H.17.d.5.0 - CAMBRAI rd. As the 3rd Divn did not advance & guard a line H.17.c.r.o - H.17.c.5.5. their line was echeloned in rear of right 110th Bde.

4.30 p.m - An attempted counter attack was made on the right flank of 110th Bde by the enemy who tried to issue from trenches about H.17.d.5.0 - 9.5. (possibly road running due S. of GUEMAPPE). This attack was dispersed by 3 Lewis guns of Bn K.R.R. & M.G. of 110th M.G.C. A Vickers gun & 2 Hotchkiss guns of cavalry cooperated from S. of CAMBRAI Rd, at about 17.d.5.7. About half hearted repetition took place at 9 p.m which was easily repulsed.

12.4.17. Battn relieved by 11th Madras Regt of 36th Bde & moved to B.O.'s O.B. BOYES.

13.4.17 Signed [illegible]

War Diary
6th (S) Bn Bedfordshire Regt

Vol. III   No. V

WAR DIARY
or
INTELLIGENCE SUMMARY.
(Erase heading not required.)

Army Form C. 2118.

Instructions regarding War Diaries and Intelligence Summaries are contained in F.S. Regs., Part II and the Staff Manual respectively. Title pages will be prepared in manuscript.

Hour, Date, Place	Summary of Events and Information	Remarks and references to Appendices
1.5.17. BERLENCOURT.	Work of reorganising battalion continued.	
2.5.17.	Battalion started training.	
9.5.17.	Divl Transport Competition won by battn by 87 points from all other regiments in the division.	
	Army Field Driving Competition open to one Coy. from all regiments of the division won by A. Coy.	
14.5.17.	Lt. Col. J.H. Edwards M.C. transferred to Home Establishment for three months rest. Lt Col W.R. Campion M.P. took command of the battalion.	
15.5.17.	Battn won Brigade Band Competition.	
18.5.17. MONTENESCOURT.	Battn moved to billets at MONTENESCOURT.	
19.5.17. TILLOY.	Battn moved to trenches at TILLOY, relieving 3rd London Regt. 168th Bde 56th Divn becoming part of the Bde in support.	
20.5.17. Support trenches	112th Bde relieved 167th Bde, 56th Divn in front line trenches from the COJEUL RIVER (O.14.c.1.1.) to O.8.a.8.9. (Ref. Map. 51.B. S.W. 1/20000) Battn relieved 1st London Regt. in trenches from N.17.d. 7.3. to N.11.b.9.2. becoming battn in Bde Support.	
21.5.17.	Hostile artillery active on-support trenches in the morning.	
	Casualties 2 killed +8 wounded.	
	Much work done in the way of salvage + improvement of trenches.	
22.5.17.	Very heavy shelling by hostile artillery towards evening, followed by gas shell bombardment at night.	
	Casualties 7 killed +14 wounded.	
	Lt.Col Edwards, Capt Blake, Capt Williams +Lt. Hislop mentioned in despatches.	
23.5.17.	Quieter day.	
24.5.17. Frontline trenches	Took over left sector of Bde front from 8th E. Lan. Regt.	

WAR DIARY
or
INTELLIGENCE SUMMARY.
(Erase heading not required.)

Army Form C. 2118.

Instructions regarding War Diaries and Intelligence Summaries are contained in F.S. Regs., Part II. and the Staff Manual respectively. Title pages will be prepared in manuscript.

Hour, Date, Place		Summary of Events and Information	Remarks and references to Appendices
TRENCHES.	25.5.17.	Hostile artillery active all day especially towards Evening. Very quiet who front line. Considerable work done in the way of salvage & improvement of trenches.	
	26.5.17.	A quiet day. A strong party was sent out at midnight 26/27 under 2/Lt CRANSWICK & WRIGT to obtain a prisoner if possible & get information about the line of shell holes held by the enemy in O.14.b.b. Before reaching the objective, a covering party was moving in front of the line of shell holes. Our party of two enemy bomb importers as our party were considerable outburst in progress had importers as our party were considerable outburst in progress but actively encounter with bomb, rifle grenade took place. Several Germans were killed the whole enemy party appear completely frightened & surprised. Fire was opened all along the line of our party intended, all men except three regaining their trenches. Casualties were 1 offr & 3 men wounded & 3 men killed. The whole operation was conducted with great determination & was highly successful considering the opposition that was met with.	Same reference Map.
	28.5.17.	Batn relieved by 8th E. Lon. Regt & 13th Rifle Brigade & retired to billets at ACHICOURT.	
ACHICOURT	29.5.17	Total casualties during tour of duty – 49 killed & wounded. (includes two officers, included regimental details).	
	31.5.17.	Battalion moved to billets at DUISANS.	
		Fighting strength of battalion 31.5.17 – 691. I.O. in 40 military medals were allotted to the batn during the month.	

H. Cunningham
at radit for
31.5.17. O.C. 6th Bedf. Regt.

War Diary

6th Bedford

June 1917

Vol 23

SECRET

37/115

23 A

Army Form C. 2118.

WAR DIARY
or
INTELLIGENCE SUMMARY.
(Erase heading not required.)

Instructions regarding War Diaries and Intelligence Summaries are contained in F.S.Regs., Part II and the Staff Manual respectively. Title pages will be prepared in manuscript.

Place	Hour, Date	Summary of Events and Information	Remarks and references to Appendices
DUISANS	1.6.17	Battalion in training.	
	3.6.17	Batn moved to IZEL LES HAMEAU - Starting at 4.30 a.m. 2 officers + 16 O.R. arrived as reinforcements.	
IZEL	4.6.17 + 5.6.17	Batn in training.	
	6.6.17	Bde tactical scheme.	
	7.6.17	Batn moved to BOURS - Starting at 4.10 a.m.	
	8.6.17	Batn moved to DELETTE in busses.	
	9.6.17	Batn in training.	
DELETTE	10.6.17	20 O.R. reinforcements arrived.	
	11.6.17	2 officers reinforcements arrived with 12 O. Ranks.	
	12.6.17	126 O.R. arrived as reinforcements. 29.O.R	
	15/16.6.17	Training still going on. Batn continued training.	
	17.6.17	Bde Church Parade + Sports. Batn very successful at heated won practically all the events.	
	19.6.17	Batn digging scheme under 153. Coy. R.E.	
	20.6.17	Officers mess dinner to celebrate the winning of the Silver bugle inefficiency competition 9th April 1917.	
	23.6.17	Batn moved to LES CISEAUX.	
	24.6.17	" " MONDEGHEM.	
	25.6.17	" " LOCRE	
LOCRE	28.6.17	Bde inspected by Army Commander.	

Army Form C. 2118.

WAR DIARY
or
INTELLIGENCE SUMMARY.
(Erase heading not required.)

Instructions regarding War Diaries and Intelligence Summaries are contained in F.S. Regs., Part II. and the Staff Manual respectively. Title pages will be prepared in manuscript.

Hour, Date, Place	Summary of Events and Information	Remarks and references to Appendices
29.6.17.	Battn relieved 12th R.I.R. (36th Divn) in Divl Reserve at KEMMEL. (N 22 a.2.4. Sheet 28. S.W. 1/20000)	
KEMMEL. 30.6.17.	Battn in Divl Reserve.	
	Strength of battn 1.6.17. 709. O.R. 30.6.17. 935. O.R.	
	Decorations awarded during the month were 5 Military Crosses, 2 D.C.M's, 1 Bar to M.M, 21 M.M's.	
	Casualties during month. Nil.	W. Cunningham. Lt & Adjt. 6/12 Bat. Reat. for O.C.

Forms/C. 2118/10.

War Diary

JULY 1917

6th BEDFORDS.

Army Form C. 2118.

WAR DIARY
or
INTELLIGENCE SUMMARY.
(Erase heading not required.)

Instructions regarding War Diaries and Intelligence Summaries are contained in F.S. Regs., Part II and the Staff Manual respectively. Title pages will be prepared in manuscript.

Hour, Date, Place		Summary of Events and Information	Remarks and references to Appendices
BAILEUL.	1.7.17	Batt'n in billets. Large working parties to front line at night.	
	3.7.17	D. Coy sent to R.E. dorm, KEMMEL for attachment to R.E. for work. Lieut D.M SAUNDERS rejoined from hospital.	
	4.7.17.	Batt'n in training.	
	5 - 8	Visit of H.M the King to 2nd Army Area. 11. O.R. arrived. reinforcements.	
	10.7.17.	Batt'n in training. Batt'n moved to KEMMEL HILL taking over camp from 8th Lincoln Regt. 112 in B'de released 63rd B'de in support.	Batt'n on a one Coy. frontage from O. 29.C. 4.0 - O. 29.C. 3.8. (R. Map. 28 S.W. 1/20000)
KEMMEL HILL.	11.7.17.	Large working parties all day. Enemy aeroplanes very active - four of our balloons brought down E. of KEMMEL.	
	12.7.17.	Capt A T Hilton rejoined & took over B. Coy.	
	13 - 15	Large working parties all day & night. Reconnoitering parties to front line.	
	18.7.17	Capt. G. Peel killed whilst on a reconnoitering party.	
	19.7.17.	Relieved 10th York & Lancs. Regt in the right sub sector of B'de front. Intermittent shelling all day - very heavy on the front line during the night.	
Trenches.	20.7.17.	2 officers arrived as reinforcements. Fairly quiet day - a lot of gas shells Casualties - 2 killed, 3 Wounded.	
	21.7.17.	Heavy shelling all day. A lot of men feeling effects of new gas used by the enemy.	
	22.7.17.	Thirty men evacuated suffering from gas - some very bad cases. Casualties, 2 killed, 1r Wounded.	
	23.7.17.	Inter Coy. reliefs at night.	

WAR DIARY
or
INTELLIGENCE SUMMARY.
(Erase heading not required.)

Army Form C. 2118.

Instructions regarding War Diaries and Intelligence Summaries are contained in F.S. Regs., Part II. and the Staff Manual respectively. Title pages will be prepared in manuscript.

Place	Hour, Date.	Summary of Events and Information	Remarks and references to Appendices
Dickebos.	24.7.17.	Hostile aeroplanes very active in the early morning. Heavy shelling at times during the day. Casualties. 1 Killed, 1 Wounded, 5 gassed. 3 officers arrived - reinforcements.	
	25.7.17	Batn relieved by 10th York & Lancs. Regt. & returned to camp on KEMMEL HILL. Casualties. 1 Killed, 1 Wounded. 5 gassed.	
KEMMEL HILL	26.7.17.	Batn to billets near BAILLEUL relieving 13th K.R.R.C.	
BAILLEUL.	27.7.17 - 30.7.17	Large working parties to front line at night.	
	30.7.17	Batn completed two years service in France.	

W. Cunningham
Lt & adjt for
Major Commdg 6th East. Regt.

WO 25

War Diary
6th Bedfords
Aug 1917

WAR DIARY
or
INTELLIGENCE SUMMARY.
(Erase heading not required.)

Army Form C. 2118.

Instructions regarding War Diaries and Intelligence Summaries are contained in F.S. Regs., Part II and the Staff Manual respectively. Title pages will be prepared in manuscript.

Place	Hour, Date	Summary of Events and Information	Remarks and references to Appendices
BAILLEUL.	1.8.17.	Battn in billets at JILLE FARM near BAILLEUL. Weather very bad.	
	2.8.17.	Battn moved to camp on KEMMEL HILL relieving 8th Lincoln Regt.	
KEMMEL.	3/4.8.17.	Battn in camp at KEMMEL. Weather still very bad indeed. Large working parties du the front line.	
	5.8.17.	Major J.A. Mackenzie to hospital - sick. Capt A.T. Hitch took over the duties of 2nd in Command. 2/Lt C.E. Kirk + 4 O.R. killed + 4 O.R. wounded on a working party.	
	6.8.17.	Battn moved to support area at ROSSIGNOL WOOD.	O.11. G.2.1 - O.17. G.3.0. (Sheet 28. S.W. 1/20000)
	7.8.17.	Battn took over the front line held by the 57th Inf Bde 19th Division relieving the 10th R War Regt + 8th Gloucester Regt. 2/Lt R. Caldwell - Cook + 9 O.R. wounded.	
Trenches.	8.8.17.	Hostile artillery active throughout the day. 20. R. killed, 20. R. wounded.	
	9.8.17.	Very heavy shelling at intervals particular near GREEN WOOD. Capt. J.G.B. Lucas M.C. killed 4 1. O.R. 3. O.R. wounded.	
	10.8.17.	5 O.R. wounded. Quieter day.	
	11.8.17.	Brig General R.C. MACLACHLAN D.S.O. killed. 2. O.R. killed, 3 O.R. wounded. Battn relieved by 8th E. Lan Regt & returned to support at DAMM STRASSE.	
	12.8.17.	Large working parties for front line. Capt. R.C. CARTHEW rejoined.	

Army Form C. 2118.

WAR DIARY
or
INTELLIGENCE SUMMARY.
(Erase heading not required.)

Instructions regarding War Diaries and Intelligence Summaries are contained in F.S. Regs., Part II. and the Staff Manual respectively. Title pages will be prepared in manuscript.

Place	Hour, Date	Summary of Events and Information	Remarks and references to Appendices
Trenches	13.8.17.	1. O.R. wounded. 20 officers arrived reinforcements.	
	14.8.17.	4 O.R. wounded. Large working parties to the front line.	
	15.8.17.	1 O.R. killed. Battⁿ relieved by 63rd Bde & battⁿ by 1/4 Middlesex. Battⁿ returned to camp near SIEGE FARM.	
SIEGE FARM.	16.8.17.	Bⁿ General A.E. IRVINE D.S.O. took command of the Bde.	
	17/19.8.17	Battⁿ in rest.	
	17.8.17	12 O.R. reinforcements arrived.	
	20.8.17.	112 hqs relieved 63rd Bde in the line. The battⁿ relieving the 8th Lincoln. Regt. in the same sector as that which it held previously. 1 O.R. killed, 1 wounded.	
		5 O.R. reinforcements arrived.	
Trenches	22.8.17.	Very quiet day. 1 O.R. killed, 1 O.R. wounded.	Some excellent patrol work done in Ypt Rogers + 2 men
	23.8.17.	do. 1 O.R. killed, 1 O.R. wounded.	of C⁰ in during this period.
	24.8.17.	Battⁿ relieved by 8th E. Lan. Regt. + returned to support at DAMM STRASSE & 1 O.R. wounded	
	26.8.17.	Heavy shelling of DAMM STRASSE at 8.30 a.m. Large working parties to front line at night.	
	27.8.17.	Bde relieved by 166th Bde. Battⁿ relieved by 1/5th R. Dublin. Returned to support area at CHINESE WALL.	
CHINESE WALL.	28.8.17.	8 O.R. reinforcements arrived.	
	29.8.17.	Battⁿ moved back to KEMMEL SHELTERS. (N.19.d.5.5.). 5 officers arrived reinforcements.	

W. Cunningham
Caper Adjt.
for O.C. 1st Reg.

Vol 26

War Diary
6th Bedfords
Sept 1917

Army Form C. 2118.

WAR DIARY
or
INTELLIGENCE SUMMARY.
(Erase heading not required.)

Instructions regarding War Diaries and Intelligence Summaries are contained in F.S. Regs., Part II and the Staff Manual respectively. Title pages will be prepared in manuscript.

Place	Hour, Date	Summary of Events and Information	Remarks and references to Appendices
KEMMEL SHELTERS	1.9.17	Orders to relieve 3/4th Division.	
	2.9.17	Batt relieved 12th Sussex & 8th Buffs & took over front line from I.36.d.5.0 – J.31.d.2.q. (Ref. Map SHRENSBURY FOREST sheet) Hdqrs in railway cutting at Hilbo.	
TRENCHES	3.9.17	Very quiet day. One petty officer & 8 sailors attached to the batt for 24 hrs.	
	4.9.17	Quiet day. Enemy attempted raid on trenches E of KLEIN ZILLEBEKE but was driven off by rifle fire. A.Coy, under 2/Lt R.H. Wright, who was slightly wounded did very well on this occasion were mainly instrumental in bringing about the failure of the raid. A patrol sent out after the raid brought in a dead hun who provided a valuable identification. One enemy came over in some strength & were provided with explosive charges.	
	5.9.17	Heavy shelling of back areas all day. Capt L.B. Beal M.C. posted to the batt as Major & 2nd in command.	
	7.9.17	Batt relieved by 10th K.O.Yorks Regt & became batt in Brigade support.	
	8/9.9.17	Batt in support. Large working parties at night to the front line.	
	10.9.17	I.O.R. reinforcements arrived. Attempted raid on enemy trenches in J.31.c by B.Coy under 2/Lt D.W. Wright, a proved a complete failure owing to the artillery shooting short & putting the barrage between ourselves & our objective. Fortunately no casualties.	
	11.9.17	Batt relieved by 10th Worcesters & 8th Staffs & withdrew to camp at SIEGE FARM. Moved back to camp near NESTOUTRE at night.	
NESTOUTRE	12.9.17	Batt in rest. 2/Lt J.C. Rogers rejoined from hospital. I.O.R. reinforcement arrived.	
	14.9.17	Working parties in back area all day.	
	16.9.17	Church parade & holiday for the batt.	
	17.9.17	Working parties all day in back area.	
	19.9.17	Bde communication scheme in afternoon. Inspection by the Brigadier after which the following letter was received from the Bde Major:- "One Bde Commander desires me to inform you that he was more than satisfied with the splendid turnout of your batt on parade this morning. The cleanliness of every article of kit as well as the general turnout spoke well for the organisation within your batt & gave him a credit to all concerned. It gave the Bde Commander very great pleasure to see such a fine parade. He feels confident that in any part the action his batt will continue to show as it has in the past half that good interior economy & organisation are half the battle.	

(73989) W4141–463. 400,000. 9/14. H.&J.Ltd. Forms/C.2118/10.

WAR DIARY
or
INTELLIGENCE SUMMARY.
(Erase heading not required.)

Army Form C. 2118.

Place	Hour, Date	Summary of Events and Information	Remarks and references to Appendices
R.E. FARM.	19.9.17.	Battn moved up at night to R.E. FARM.	
	20.9.17.	10551. Cpl S.W. Sawford awarded the Military Medal. General attack on Army front. Battn not used - battn remained at R.E. FARM.	
	21.9.17.	Battn moved back to WESTOUTRE. 20 O.R. reinforcements arrived.	
WESTOUTRE	22.9.17.	Battn relieved 39th Divn – (6 Cheshires) – in front line at 5 hrs notice. Taken up in busses. Extremely difficult relief + battn heavily shelled on the way up. Capt J. Hislop M.C. + 2/Lt C.E. Inch killed + H.O.R., 20 O.R. wounded. Took over line J.26.c.9.4 – J.26.d.6.9.	
TRENCHES	23.9.17.	Very heavy shelling all day, but only 2 O.R. wounded.	
	24.9.17.	Heavy shelling continued. 20.R killed, 7 wounded. Relieved at night by 10th K.O.N. Lan. Regt. Became battn in bde support.	
	25.9.17.	Continued shelling. 2/Lt N.W. Ryecroft + 11 O.R. killed, 16 O.R. wounded. 4 O.R. CARRE + 200 O.R. arrived as reinforcements. Battn maintained an unbeaten record in coolies rhubarb competition at 37th Divl Horse Show held near ST JEAN CAPEL.	
	26.9.17.	General attack on the left continued. Hostile artillery very active all day. 6 O.R. wounded.	
	27.9.17.	Hostile artillery considerably diminished + a much quieter day altogether.	
R.E. FARM.	28.9.17.	Battn relieved by 10th Worcesters. (19th Division), + returned to R.E. FARM. Battn moved into Divl Reserve at BOIS CARRE. Hostile aircraft active at night - several bombs dropped.	
BOIS CARRE	29.9.17.	Battn resting. 5 Officers joined reinforcements.	

W. Cunningham
Capt & adjt
for O.C. 6th Bn R. Regt

War Diary
of
1st (Service) Battalion Bedfordshire Regiment.
From 1st October 1917 To 31st October 1917

VOLUME 26

Army Form C. 2118.

WAR DIARY
or
INTELLIGENCE SUMMARY.
(Erase heading not required.)

Instructions regarding War Diaries and Intelligence Summaries are contained in F.S. Regs., Part II and the Staff Manual respectively. Title pages will be prepared in manuscript.

Place	Hour, Date	Summary of Events and Information	Remarks and references to Appendices
BOIS CARRÉ	1/10/17	Batt. resting. 2nd Lt F.J. Blake was 2.O.Rs. misfortunate arrived	
	2/10/17	21 O.Rs. reinforcements arrived. Officers reconnoitre routes to trenches.	
	3/10/17	Batt. still resting, warm weather. Received two O.Rs. wounded, attached R.E.	
TRENCHES	4/10/17	Batt. to trenches at 2.0pm. C/Spl & Sgt. H.J. Cunningham killed. 2nd Lt C.C. Clifford wounded. 2 O.Rs. wounded. Batt. relief by 63rd and 115th Batts. spent the night in trenches near Mt. Sorrel.	
	5/10/17	R.M. Att. C. enjoined upon return to H.Q. via S-9 Menin-Ypres Rd., guides sent to meet returning Rcts. to N.Q. by 10th Van Lawes Regt. to Militia Lodge on 8th Lincolns. Batt. relieved these Regts. with first line J.26-A.60.10, J.26-A.90-75 walkie hung shelling... suffered casualties from Batt. Headquarters... difficulties... rail... until daylight, possibly damaged 2 O.Rs. killed 8 O.Rs. wounded	
	6/10/17	Ran fresh'ing. gas shells fired, French front took. Very little effort. Campion who was left behind by way of the Brigade came up command taken. Lieut Heron rejoined from trench Duvers as adjutant.	
	7/10/17	12202 Pt. Dickinson 10th Upper Green wounded. He Midshm were called by Artillery bombarded the German front line throughout the day with small, small, our first line was withdrawn to the support and in rear of the Brigade, at night the enemy attempted to lift us out patrols found Germans in advance of our line. Pt. enemy was still shelling full same positions. He was ... 10-O.Rs. killed 15 O.Rs. wounded	
	8/10/17	A very quiet day. Wired with front line; but seemed shelling near Batt. Headquarters. 1 O.R. killed 11 O.R. wounded 2.0 OR. missing 2 O.Rs. killed 12 O.Rs. wounded. ENEMY made a voluntary retirement. General advance on army front. Evening Lt. Pratt & Bademay... wounded, 11 OR wounded 2 ORs missing. The which had not moved from Sunn scene shelling grounds. 10 Rounded. Killed & 4 O.Rs. wounded & 2 Lt CRIVEN wounded. 1 O.R. killed 2nd Lt ROBINSON & English taking. Broke 1 minute every just one 6 OR wounded 2nd Lt. ... suffering from the ...	
	9/10/17	A quiet day spent by the Artillery barrage. 2nd Lt CRIVEN wounded. 1 O.R. killed 2nd Lt ROBINSON & English for 6 months. Handed filled in the 8th S.L.I. (63rd Brig.), company shelling in the Lock Sheet... hand of duty. Guns from Spoilbank to Little Kemmel Camp. Batt. unduly Guances suffering Batt. cent off an evening road with for comfort	
LITTLE KEMMEL	10/8/17	Retiring at LITTLE KEMMEL.	
	11/10/17	Resting. Lt. Col. CAMPION to ENGLAND on 6 months leave.	
	12/10/17	Batt. at EPSOM CAMP NEAR WEST OUTRE 1 O.R. wounded, attack R.E.	
	13/10/17	Batt. resting. 2nd Lt J. BLAKELEY misfortunate	
	14/10/17	8 officers 250 O.Rs. to YPRES for work on roads in ANZAC Corps area. H.Q.s Americans EPSOM CAMP. 256 O.Rs. under the command of the 11th West Warwicks Regt.	
WEST OUTRE	15/10/17	Lt E.S. AYER and 90 misfortunate arrive. Details left at EPSOM CAMP start training.	
WEST OUTRE and YPRES	16/10/17	Enemy bomb camp NEAR YPRES where the working party stops. No casualties	
	17/10/17	2nd Lt S. VAN DEL LINDE killed & W.A. POLL and 3 O.Rs wounded, by bombs dropped by E.A. in E.G.) YPRES	
	18/10/17	Training carried on in EPSOM CAMP as usual	

WAR DIARY
or
INTELLIGENCE SUMMARY
(Erase heading not required.)

Army Form C. 2118.

Instructions regarding War Diaries and Intelligence Summaries are contained in F.S. Regs., Part II. and the Staff Manual respectively. Title Pages will be prepared in manuscript.

Place	Date	Hour	Summary of Events and Information	Remarks and references to Appendices
WEST OUTRE	19/10/17		Batt. Hqrs and outside at SPION CAMP. 25 ORs at YPRES. 25 ORs sick for wounds	
	20/10/17		ditto. Two officers sent up to replace casualties at YPRES.	
	21/10/17		2nd Lt A. STONE M.C. 2nd Lt F. SMITH wd. ORs wd sick/wounds	
	22/10/17		275 ORs returned from YPRES, inspected & all drafts by C.O.	
	23/10/17		All men returned from YPRES bathing. Remainder parading from 9 am to 12.30 pm	
BERTHEN	24/10/17		Batt. moves to billets in BERTHEN. 3800 in billets. Remainder in barns. 50 men carried on busses & suffering with Trench feet	
	25/10/17		Training begin. 2nd Lts for Company 11772 Cpl. LOREN, 12001 L/Cpl F LEE, 32120 L/Cpl R GRUBB, 16434 L/Cpl H WRIGHT, 43225 Pte G SMITH awarded the Military Medal	
	26/10/17		Lt Col G. L. COURTNEY annual. Estate command of the Batt.	
LOCRE	27/10/17		Batt. marched to DONCASTER HUTS in LOCRE	
	28/10/17		Training Hqrs carried on	
	29/10/17		2nd Lt W. WRIGHT, 2nd Lt A WALLER, 2nd Lt ARTABOR, 2nd Lt BLAVINSKY wounded, 1 OR killed, 4 ORs wounded (2 at duty) by bomb 2nd Lt A) which exploded inside 'B' Coy. officers Mess. Training carried on	
	30/10/17		Inter Batt. Transport competition. The Batt took first place. Training carried on	
	31/10/17		Inter Batt. Drum competition. The Batt took second place. 2nd Lt. E F ASHBY awarded the Military Cross.	

J M Saunders H. ay adj
for Lt. Colonel
Commanding 6 Bt (S) 13th Bedfordshire Reg.

WAR DIARY
or
INTELLIGENCE SUMMARY.

(Erase heading not required.)

Army Form C. 2118.

6 Bedfordshire

Hour, Date, Place	Summary of Events and Information	Remarks and references to Appendices
Locat. 1/11/17	Battn. resting at home. Training carried on.	
" 2/11/17	Battn. resting at home. Training carried on.	
" 3/11/17	"	
" 4/11/17	Who fell in the fighting from 5/10/17 to 11/10/17. 2. O.R. reinforcements arrived. Brigade memorial service for all thro' the firm Lorraine and Humber of the Battn. Brigade rugby XV beat 42nd Squadron - lost 12 - Nil. Warning order to press up the line in the 8th.	
" 5/11/17	Battn. resting and training carried on.	
" 6/11/17	Bn. resting and training carried on. C.O. visits the line that Battn. has to take over 8th.	
" 7/11/17	Battn. training - 6 O.R. reinforcements arrived.	
"	Battn. prepare to move up the line on 8/11/17. 9 n.k. Brigade transport completed in. 6th Brigade relieved 112 Lt Bde. H12 Bde with the competition and preserved 400 francs on prize for games.	
Bois Confluent 8/11/17	Battn. moved to Bois Confluent, absence parties reconnoitred the line using the night in the line. Hilobrunner of 57th Rde. P.I.2.90.31. J.32.A.65.80 J.26.b.27.28 Hollisekerke 1/10,000. The sector	
Line 9/11/17	Batt. to line. Relieving trenches from 8th Gloucester Reg. the Battn. then went I. O.R. killed 3. O.R. wounded very much quieter than any trenches previously held by the Battn. then year.	
" 10/11/17	A quiet day. great difficulty experienced obtaining information. men set in, but great deal of work 1. O.R. wounded. All 4 companies in the line. Battn. sector now run from J.32.a.85.80 to J.26.b.27.28. Men left are very well off, with five dryness right	
" 11/11/17	The two Southern coys relieved by 8th E hams night. quick, comfortable until dawn. Still two (one officer) remain until day.	
" 12/11/17	A coy: no great case of enemy sniping. Boches very quiet all day.	
" 13/11/17	B coy relieved by HI coy in the right coy sector.	
" 14/11/17	Very quiet day, a certain amount of sniping, artillery fire very little.	
" 15/11/17	A coy relieved by C coy in the right sector. 'A' coy on the left remains in front the whole 8 days.	
" 16/11/17	A coy relieved by our own train. no casualties suffered. a great deal of salvage work done by the reserve coy at Corner House. 13th RA Coy reconnoitring parts up the line with to Battn. with line on the night 17/18 November.	

Army Form C. 2118.

WAR DIARY
or
INTELLIGENCE SUMMARY.
(Erase heading not required.)

Instructions regarding War Diaries and Intelligence Summaries are contained in F.S. Regs., Part II and the Staff Manual respectively. Title pages will be prepared in manuscript.

Hour, Date, Place	Summary of Events and Information	Remarks and references to Appendices
B Line 17/9/17	Battn. in trenches arrived by Rly. 13th R.B. very backward. Chiefly owing to the bad state of the ground. Carparks Steam. 2/Lt Offer for fatigue.	
Bois Confluent 18/9/17	Battn. to Bois Confluent. 180 O.R.s on 2/officer for fatigue.	
19/9/17	230 o.r.s and 7 offrs on fatigue. 1 o.r. wounded.	
20/9/17	Capt. Hatch to 11th Warwickshire Regt. on 2/c command – 240 o.r.s and 7 officers for fatigue – taking over new area.	
21/9/17	Fatigue – great difficulty in finding men.	
22/9/17	5 o.r.s out on fatigue. Afternoon – aeroplane above – dropped about 50 bombs. No damage done to the Battn.	
23/9/17	Enemy bombs medium guns.	
24/9/17	Aeroplane on above. Fatigue on usual.	
Tournai Camp 25/9/17	Battn. to Tournai Camp nr Vierstraat. Very improved camp – not quite finished. Fatigue found to mend.	
26/9/17	Platn. have baths and clean up. No uniform. No. 241034 Pte Newby appeared to Military M.E. 2/Lt. Ce Ellifford, 2/Lt. H.D. Gates, 2/Lt. F. Gooling up to join unit.	
27/9/17	2/Lt F.C. Cook R.F.C. on probation one month out on furlough – an enormous number.	
28/9/17	2/Lt. Plaston to hospital ill appendicitis. Into Platoon further completion quickly advance sideways.	
29/9/17	Battr. at – Siding work. Into platoon further completion	
30/9/17	Battr. out on fatigue for R.E.'s round the camp. No having trouble; wk.	
1/1/17	Platoon further further completion.	

H.W. Gordon 2 Lt. 9/9/17
J.M.O.C. 6th Bn. Bedfordshire Regt.

WAR DIARY or INTELLIGENCE SUMMARY

Army Form C. 2118.

6 Bedfords

Hour, Date, Place	Summary of Events and Information	Remarks and references to Appendices
1st December 1917 TOURNAI CAMP.	Batt'n in reserve at TOURNAI CAMP. Working parties.	
2nd "	Batt'n in reserve; training. Divisional guard to transport in celebration of winning the Divisional Competition.	
3rd "	Working parties. Great difficulty in finding sufficient number of men.	
4th "	Training at TOURNAI CAMP. 5 O.R's reinforcements arrived.	
5th Trenches	Batt'n to trenches. Very quiet relief; completed 9.0 p.m. owing to hard state of ground.	
6th "	Very quiet day. 2 prisoners captured. One wounded by a 2nd Coy sentry; not having answered the challenge.	
7th "	Front line shelled a little. Otherwise very quiet.	
8th "	Very quiet day. Ground become very hard owing to thaw.	
9th "	Great difficulty experienced carrying parties owing to bad state of the ground.	
10th "	Great difficulty experienced by carrying parties owing to bad state of ground. Weather very cold; an intense frost, frozen ground stored seen sufficient	
11th "	Very quiet day.	
12th "	Very quiet day. Has rendered difficulty for working parties. 2nd Lieut Lumsden joined. 2nd Lieut H. Brigden	
13th SPOILBANK.	Batt'n moved to dugouts = SPOILBANK- forward Batt'n. 2nd Lieut H. Brigden Resting.	
14th "	Whole Batt'n on working parties. Lts H J. GREIG, T. PEMBERTON 2nd Lts H. SKEEP	
15th "	W A S Officer. A. E. WARNECKE joined the Batt'n for duty.	
16th "	Working parties. 1 O.R. Killed. 1 O.R. died of wounds. 2 O.Rs wounded	
17th "	Working parties.	
18th "	Working parties.	

37/T/2

Army Form C. 2118.

WAR DIARY
or
INTELLIGENCE SUMMARY.
(Erase heading not required.)

Instructions regarding War Diaries and Intelligence Summaries are contained in F.S. Regs., Part II and the Staff Manual respectively. Title pages will be prepared in manuscript.

Hour, Date, Place	Summary of Events and Information	Remarks and references to Appendices
19th December SPOILBANK	Working parties. 12 OR reinforcements arrive. 1 OR wounded	
20th "	Working parties.	
21st " CURRAGH CAMP	Batt. to CURRAGH CAMP. 83 OR reinforcements arrive. 3 OR wounded en route for parties.	
22nd "	Major F H EDWARDS MC arrived & takes over command of Batt.	
23rd "	Working parties	
24th "	Batt. training	
25th "	Resting. Christmas dinner for men - great success	
26th "	Batt. training	
27th "	Working parties - a case of accidental discharge used. Officers reconnoitre new sector of line.	
28th "	17 OR reinforcements arrive. Batt. left on working parties	
29th "	Batt. to trenches, takes over night sector 4th Division's front. from CANAL BANK to HOLLEBEKE (exclusive). Relief difficult owing to chalky + show on the ground single shelling	
30th "	2 OR killed, 3 OR wounded.	
31st "	Quiet day.	

FMSawyer
Capt & A/A Bedf R
for OC
6th B.

probably
1918

6 Bedford Regt

309

WAR DIARY
or
INTELLIGENCE SUMMARY.
(Erase heading not required.)

Army Form C. 2118.

Hour, Date, Place	Summary of Events and Information	Remarks and references to Appendices
1st January 1917. TRENCHES	Battn in the line near HOLLEBEKE	
2nd "	Battn Hdqrs heavily shelled with Gas Shells - two men wounded	
3rd "	Quiet day.	
4th "	Quiet day.	
5th "	Battn relieved - Moved to support in TOURNAI CAMP - 2nd Lt. W. A. SODGEN and 2 O.R. wounded.	
6th TOURNAI CAMP	Resting	
7th "	Working parties.	
8th "	Working parties - 10 reinforcements	
9th "	Transport moved to SERCUS AREA via STRAZEELE	
10th "	Battn entrained DICKEBUSH - Detrained EBBLINGHAM marched to billets in SERCUS.	
11th SERCUS	Training	
12th "	Training	
13th "	Training - Weather bad	
14th "	Training - Weather very bad	
15th "	Training - Heavy Gale.	
16th "	Training - 1 Drummer killed owing to barn collapsing.	
17th "	Training - Weather Bad	
18th "	Training	
19th "	Training	
Sunday "	(Training Inspection of the Battn by Divisional Commander & G.O.C. Brigade	
20th "	Transport moved to forward area.	
21st "	Battn entrained EBBLINGHAM - detrained DICKEBUSCH marched to huts at MAIDA CAMP.	

Army Form C. 2118.

WAR DIARY
or
INTELLIGENCE SUMMARY.
(Erase heading not required.)

Instructions regarding War Diaries and Intelligence Summaries are contained in F.S. Regs., Part II. and the Staff Manual respectively. Title pages will be prepared in manuscript.

Hour, Date, Place	Summary of Events and Information	Remarks and references to Appendices
22nd Jany. MAIDA CAMP.	Working parties - 1 OR Killed 8 wounded including 1 at duty	
23rd "	Working parties 10R wounded	
24th "	Working parties	
24th "	2nd Lt D H WHITEHOUSE to ENGLAND for Tank Corps.	
25th "	Working parties	
26th "	Working parties	
27th "	Resting - Lt BARNARD L.E. to 153rd Field Coy for duty	
28th "	Working parties	
29th "	Working parties - 1 OR wounded	
30th "	Working parties	
31st "	Working parties	

31.1.18

J.F.Edmonds Lt. Col.
Cmdg. 6th Rl of Regt.

Confidential

War Diary.

of

6th Battalion Bedfordshire Regt.

from

February 1st 1918

to

February 28th 1918

Volume 31.

Army Form C. 2118.

WAR DIARY
or
INTELLIGENCE SUMMARY.
(Erase heading not required.)

Instructions regarding War Diaries and Intelligence Summaries are contained in F. S. Regs., Part II. and the Staff Manual respectively. Title pages will be prepared in manuscript.

Place	Date	Hour	Summary of Events and Information	Remarks and references to Appendices
MAIDA CAMP	1/2/18		Working Parties. 1 Man wounded.	
"	2.2.18		Working Parties.	
"	3.2.18		Working Parties. 1 O.R. wounded. 2nd Lieut. PLOWRIGHT struck off Strength	
"	4.2.18		Entrained DICKEBUSCH - Detrained EBBINGHAM + marched to billets in HEURINGHEM.	
BILLETS HEURINGHEM	5.2.18		Training. 2nd Lt. MAS.OGDEN transferred to ENGLAND wounded.	
"	6.2.18		Training - 2nd Lt G.A BURNS joined the Battn from 1st H.A.C.	
"	7.2.18		Training	
"	8.2.18		Training. 96 O.R.s joined the Battn as reinforcements. Off Reinforcements 2nd Lieuts HADFIELD, L.S. P.A. O'SULLIVAN, J.W. DRUMMOND, E.R.S. WHITE.	
"	9.2.18		Training.	
"	10.2.18		CHURCH PARADE. 115 O.Rs (reinforcements) from 8th Battn Bedford Regt joined the Battn. officer reinforcements Capt A.W. ELLIOT. M.C. 2nd Lt. H. WILLIAMS, 2nd Lt. W.O. WILSON. (from 8th Battn Bedf Regt.)	
"	11.2.18		Training.	
"	12.2.18		Training. 10. O.R. (reinforcement) joined Battn from 8th Bedford Regt. officer reinforcement from 6th BEDF. Regt. Lt H.W. CLARK. Major G.W. COURTNEY left Battn for ENGLAND.	
"	13.2.18		Training -	
"	14.2.18		Training -	
" CAMP	15.2.18		Marched to EBBINGHAM and entrained for DICKEBUSCH. marched to MALPLAQUET CAMP.	
MALPLAQUET	16.2.18		Battn moved to front line (POLDER HOEK SECTOR) Battn H.Q. yrs STIRLING CASTLE	
Trenches	17.2.18		In Trenches. 1 O.R. wounded.	
Trenches	18.2.18		In Trenches. 1 O.R. wounded (at duty). officer reinforcement from 8th Battn. BEDF.R. 2nd Lt. R. BLAND.	
"	19.2.18		In Trenches.	
"	20.2.18		In Trenches. 3 O.R.s wounded.	
"	21.2.18		Battn moved to Reserve MAIDA CAMP.	
MAIDA CAMP.	22.2.18		BEDFORD REGT. NIGHT working parties. 1 O.R. wounded -	

Army Form C. 2118.

WAR DIARY
or
INTELLIGENCE=SUMMARY.
(Erase heading not required.)

Place	Date	Hour	Summary of Events and Information	Remarks and references to Appendices
MAIDA CAMP	23.2.18		Resting - 2nd Lt D.KEW. DCM. M.M. reinforcement from Royal BERKSHIRE REGT	
"	24.2.18		Church Parade -	
"	25.2.18		Training	
"	26.2.18		Battn moved into front line (MENIN ROAD SECTOR)	
IN TRENCHES	27.2.18		In Trenches - Officer reinforcements from 8th Battn Bedf.R. Lt H.W.WRIGHT. 2/Lt WAMBRIDGE	
"	28.2.18		In Trenches - 1 OR Killed. 6 OR Wounded.	

F.A. Edwards. Lt. Col.
Commanding 6th(S) Battn Bedf Regt

WAR DIARY
of
6th BEDFORD REGT
for
MARCH 1918

VOLUME XXI

Army Form C. 2118.

WAR DIARY
or
INTELLIGENCE SUMMARY.
(Erase heading not required.)

Instructions regarding War Diaries and Intelligence Summaries are contained in F. S. Regs., Part II. and the Staff Manual respectively. Title pages will be prepared in manuscript.

Place	Date	Hour	Summary of Events and Information	Remarks and references to Appendices
Front line	1st March		Front line - Enemy artillery lively	
do.	2nd "		Front line - 2 O.Rs gassed 1. Off (2Lt H.Williams) + 1. other rank wounded -	
"	3rd "		Front line - Quiet.	
"	4th "		Front line - Quiet. Battn relieved by 13th Bn R.Fusiliers moved to Support.	
			4. other ranks wounded -	
Trenches	5th "		In Support - Quiet.	
"	6th "		In Support. 29. other Ranks reinforcements	
"	7th "		In Support. Quiet	
"	8th "		Enemy put down heavy barrage throughout the day + attacked 111th Bde front at 5.30 p.m. S.O.S. sent up on the divisional front. Enemy gained a footing in the left sector but were ejected before dawn -	
"	9th "		Fairly quiet.	
"	10th "		Quiet -	
"	11th "		Battn moved back into reserve at MAIDA CAMP. 1. other Rank wounded -	
MAIDA CAMP	12th "		Battn resting -	
	13th "		Work done on Camp - bombproofing huts - Battn football team beat Divnl H.Q. 4 - 1	
	14th "		ditto	
	15th "		ditto	
	16th "		Battn moved to Front line + relieved 1st Battn Essex Reat -	
Trenches	17th "		Quiet. Bn Hdqrs shelled with gas	
	18th "		3. other Ranks wounded	
	19th "		1. other Rank wounded - 18 other ranks reinforcements	

Army Form C. 2118.

WAR DIARY
or
INTELLIGENCE SUMMARY.
(Erase heading not required.)

Instructions regarding War Diaries and Intelligence Summaries are contained in F. S. Regs., Part II. and the Staff Manual respectively. Title pages will be prepared in manuscript.

Place	Date	Hour	Summary of Events and Information	Remarks and references to Appendices
Trenches	20th March	21.56	Front line – 2 Other Ranks wounded – 8 O.Ranks gassed	
"	21st		do – 2 Other Ranks killed – 4 Other ranks wounded –	
"	22nd		Moved to Support + relieved 1st Bn Essex Regt.	
"	23rd		Support – 3 O.Ranks killed 2. O.R wounded – Lt J.M.HENDRIE joined Bn for duty. 2. O.Ranks reinforcements –	
	24th		Support.	
	25th		Moved to Reserve at MALPLAQUET CAMP.	
MALPLAQUET CAMP.	26th		Reserve – 51 O.Ranks Reinforcements	
	27th		Moved to BORRE by lorry. Transport moved by road.	
BORRE	28th		Battn + Transport entrained CAESTRE STN detrained MONDICOURT.	
MONDICOURT	29th		arrived MONDICOURT + marched to billets in TOOTENCOURT.	
ditto	30th		Marched to billets in COUIN.	
COUIN.	31st		Battn moved to front line – Transport + details at COUIN.	

H. Goodson 2 Lt a/adjt
for Lt/Col
Cmdg 6th Bedfordshire Regt.

112th Inf.Bde.
37th Div.

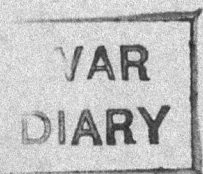

6th BATTN. THE BEDFORDSHIRE REGIMENT.

A P R I L

1 9 1 8

CONFIDENTIAL

WAR DIARY

OF

6TH BEDFORD REGT.

FROM 1ST APRIL TO 30TH APRIL

1918

VOLUME XXXII

WAR DIARY or INTELLIGENCE SUMMARY.

(Erase heading not required.)

Army Form C. 2118.

Place	Date	Hour	Summary of Events and Information	Remarks and references to Appendices
Trenches	1st April		Battn in the line. ROSSIGNOL WOOD Sector. Three Coys in front line 1 in support. Two prisoners Captured. Fairly quiet. Artillery active on "D" Coy front.	
do	2nd	"	COUIN to BAYENCOURT. Battn in line. Four O.R. Killed. Seven wounded. Transport & details moved from	
do	3rd	"	-do- Six O.R. Killed. 10 wounded.	
do	4th	"	Battn moved into support. "A" Coy sent up to reinforce left Battn at BUCQUOY. Capt L.A.H.F.W. Rees.	
do	5th	"	A Coy moved back after a bad time in line. Battn area heavily shelled from 5 AM to 9 AM. 1 OR Killed 1 man wounded + a cooker damaged at Transport line. 1 OR killed 4 wounded, 1 off + 27 OR Gassed (1 died of gas). Details & Transport moved to COUIN.	
do	6th	"	A.C. + D Coys to front line. B Coy to Support. One prisoner captured. 13 OR Killed 3 died of wounds. 29 wounded. 1 officer + 23 OR Gassed.	
do	7th	"	Front line. 8 OR wounded 1 O.R. Gassed. 21 O.R. reinforcements.	
do	8th	"	-do- 2 off (2/Lt ANSBRIDGE + 2/Lt BINNS) + 7 OR killed. 1 OR died of wounds. 1 off + 9 OR wounded.	
do.	9th	"	Battn moved to support in GOMMECOURT System. 2 OR wounded.	
GOMMECOURT	10th	"	Support. 2 ORs reinforcements.	
do	11th	"	-do- 1 OR Gassed. 4 OR reinforcements.	
do	12th	"	Battn moved to front line. ROSSIGNOL WOOD. 2 Coys in line, 2 coys in support. Very quiet indeed. 1 OR Killed 2 wounded 1 Gassed.	
Trenches	13th	"	Battn in line. quiet. 1 OR wounded.	
"	14th	"	ditto. quiet.	
"	15th	"	-do- quiet.	
"	16th	"	Battn moved to Reserve in BOIS DE WARNIMONT. 7 OR reinforcements.	
BOIS DE WARNIMONT.	17th	"	Very bad accommodation in huts. Battn resting. 55 ORs reinforcements. Battn took over from 6th Battn Cams Terr.	

Army Form C. 2118.

WAR DIARY
or
INTELLIGENCE SUMMARY.
(Erase heading not required.)

Instructions regarding War Diaries and Intelligence Summaries are contained in F. S. Regs., Part II. and the Staff Manual respectively. Title pages will be prepared in manuscript.

Place	Date	Hour	Summary of Events and Information	Remarks and references to Appendices
BOIS DE WARNIMONT	18th April		Training – 6 OR Reinforcements	
	19th	"	– do – 3 OR reinforcements. 11 off Reinforcements. Lt R.S. DENNING, 2/Lts E.M. CRAKE, A.A. WATSON	
	20th	"	A. JOLL, C.H. FLOOD, E. HARDY, E.H.I. CHANDLER, A.F. ALLEN, H.G. KAYE, P.J. HOLT, F.F. GOWLER.	
	21st		Training	
	22nd		– do –	
	23rd		– do – Lt R. ROBINSON + 4 ORs reinforcements	
	24th		Battn moved to Reserve (Bde) at FONQUEVILLERS – Transport to SOUASTRE – accommodation good on line –	
FONQUEVILLERS	25th		Battn in Reserve – 10 ORs reinforcements	
	26th		– do – Very quiet. Working parties 7 off 250 O Ranks	
	27		– do – – do – – do – 250 O Ranks	
	28		FONQUEVILLERS Shelled intermittently – – do – – do –	
	29		Very quiet – Working parties 6 off 250 O Ranks	
	30		– do – – do – – do – orders received to proceed to	
			Support RETTEMOY FARM on night 1/2nd MAY.	

H.S. Goodson
2 Lt as Adjt
for OC 6th Beds Regt.

(A8001) Wt. W1771/M291 750,000 5/17 Sch. 93 Forms C2118/14
D. D. & L. London, E.C.

TRAINING CADRE
39TH DIVISION
116TH INFY BDE

6TH BN BEDFORD REGT
MAY - JUN 1918

WAR DIARY or INTELLIGENCE SUMMARY

Army Form C. 2118.

6 Bedford 34

Place	Date	Hour	Summary of Events and Information	Remarks and references to Appendices
LINE MAILLY MAILLET	1/5/18		Batt. in support near RETTEMOY FARM - west of BUCQUOY. Working parties found. 52 ORs reinforcements. Lowell arrived.	
"	2/5/18		Batt. in support. Working parties found. Line quiet.	
"	3/5/18		- do - - do -	
"	4/5/18		Batt. in support. Line very quiet. Lieut CARLES to R.A.F. 7. ORs reinforcements arrived. Major Bevel to England on 6 mths leave.	
"	5/5/18		1. O.R. Killed by aeroplane bomb.	
"	6/5/18			
"	7/5/18		Bn. relieve 13th R. FUSILIERS in front line. S.W. of BUCQUOY. A.15 coy. front line. C. support II reserve. duty.	
"	8/5/18		S.A.A. on RETTEMOY FARM. O.R. wounded. Line very quiet. 1 prisoner captured. Most important identification. 1 AMERICAN officer attached for 2 days for distribution. 3 patrols sent out. 2nd Lts BAILEY & CHANDLER arrived. 4 ORs reinforcements arrived. L/B.G.C.E. 11/12 Inf Bde for ground patrol work.	
"	9/5/18		Line very quiet. 2 ORs wounded. 2 patrols sent out. Information reports that 18th G.R.Bn relieved by H/Ibatt. Regt.	
"	10/5/18		Line very quiet. 2 ORs wounded. Intermittently shelled. No casualties. 2 patrols sent out. T.M. activity against 15 Corps. RETTEMOY FARM Lt AUST R.E. gassed.	
"	11/5/18		Enemy shelled BEAUQUESNES LIBAR for 3 hours with gas shells. Considerably heavy.	
"	12/5/18		4. ORs wounded. 2 patrols sent out. 22 ORs attached R.E's gassed on 11/5/18 to hospital.	
"	13/5/18		RETTEMOY FRONT shelled. 1. O.R. killed. 2 patrols sent out.	
"	14/5/18		Line v. quiet. 4. ORs wounded. 2 ORs reinforcements. A patrol sent out.	
"	15/5/18		Line v. quiet. 2. ORs reinforcements. 2 patrols sent out.	
"	16/5/18		Line very quiet. 2 patrols sent out. Information received that H.Q.'s of B. be relieved by H/Ibatt. Line found quiet. 1 M.G. field, abt RETTEMOY from shell. 1. American Officer attached for instruction. 4. ORs wounded.	

2449 Wt. W14957/Mgo 750,000 1/16 J.B.C. & A. Forms/C.2118/12.

WAR DIARY or INTELLIGENCE SUMMARY

Army Form C. 2118.

Place	Date	Hour	Summary of Events and Information	Remarks and references to Appendices
LINE	17/5/18		Batt'n relieved by 2/7th & 1/West Yorks Regt. Battn relief completed midnight 17/18th. On lorry from Souastre to Louvencourt.	
LOUVENCOURT	18/5/18		Battn warned to prepare Training Staff for an American Bn. 7. ORs reinforcements. Battn clean up.	
	19/5/18		Order received that BN Gen American Training Staff will proceed to // Herts on 21/5/18. Illness prevented Brigade Staff present. No specialists sent.	
	20/5/18		Officers two farewell dinner in evening. Lt. Col. F.H. Edwards M.C. (C.O.) O/Capt H.M. Saunders (Adjt) Capt A.W. Elliott (M.C.) a/Capt Training Staff consisting of 2/Lt A.E. Iliffe (a.b. Commanders) Lt. Burgess (L.L.O) & Lt. L.O. Clifford (I.O.) O.C. No. Son. 2/Lt. W. Johnson 2/Lt A.E. Iliffe (a.b. Commanders) R.S.M. R.Q.M.S. 4 C.S.M's 4 C.Q.M.S. and 48 ORs 2/Lt W.F.E. Assay (Signals) Capt J.A.M. Hislop (Q.M.) Remainder of 83 proceeded to I/Herts Regt. Proceeded to Monzicourt. Retained for Auxurieq.	
	21/5/18		1st Bedford Regt still exists. Returned at Acurriq 1.30 pm marched to Mielles 13th R. Sussex Regt. And less for march provided on arrival. Staff very cordially received. 39th Division very complete kilestt. Rec. for all ranks on	
MIELLES	22/5/18		Specialist training from 9.0 AM to 12.30pm daily. P.M. Instruction ... Consisting of Physical training, football, hockey, running carried out each afternoon.	
	23/5/18			
	24/5/18			
	25/5/18			
	26/5/18		RAMC Bathing parade, inspection etc carried out.	
	27/5/18		Lectures by Lt. Col. F.H. Edwards M.C. to all officers.	
	28/5/18			
	29/5/18			
	30/5/18			

H. M. Saunders Capt & adjt
for Lieut. Col.
Commanding 1st Bedfordshire Regt.

6th Bedfordshire Regt
T.C.
Army Form C. 2118. 37

Vol 35

WAR DIARY
or
INTELLIGENCE SUMMARY
(Erase heading not required.)

Place	Date	Hour	Summary of Events and Information	Remarks and references to Appendices
MEULERS-LES-ATTREES	Jun 1st/18		Training Staff waiting at Neulles for 10th Amunition Regt to arrive	35 Q.
	2nd		Meanwhile 3 Officers & 12 N.C.Os report from Suffolk Regt to assist in Training 126th A. Regt.
	3rd		— do —
	4th		1st & 2nd Bn 10th Regt arrive and are stationed at ZUTKERQUE & LA MONTARE, respectively. 2 company Commanders and 12 N.C.Os instruct the 2nd Bn at NEULES. Ht. Qrs & remainder of Instructors remain at NEULLES Res Centre.
	5th		Training of 1st & 2nd Amunition Bns commences
	6th		— do —
	7th		— do —
	8th		3rd Bn. 10th Regt N°9a 10th Reg Regt expected to arrive.
	9th		Training of 1st & 2nd Bns continues
	10th		— do —
	11th		3rd Bn of Regt N°9a arrive. 3rd Bn remains NEULIET. Regt N°9a proceed to NATEAU COCOVE
	12th		Training of 3rd Bn commences
	13th		Training of 10th Regt in progress
	14th		— do —
	15th		— do —
	16th		Barrage demonstration by Divisional Artillery at MONT LEULINGHEM attended by 36th Amunition
	17th		Training continues

WAR DIARY
or
INTELLIGENCE SUMMARY

(Erase heading not required.)

Army Form C. 2118.

Place	Date	Hour	Summary of Events and Information	Remarks and references to Appendices
NIELLES-LES-ARDRES	16th Jan 18		Training of 126th Regt: Solution as far as possible. Orders received that all extended instructors rejoin their units. OC 126th Infantry adjt. have an conversation with each of the 27 NCO instructors. Names of NIELLES Sick 11/3 = 13.	
	17th		Training of 126th Inf Regt. commences. Lts CLIFFORD & ASHBY ordered to report as I.O. & Sgt Inst.	
	18th		To report to 1st Wing with School, were agreed upon which they supervised. American instruments considered for to take their respective places.	
	19th		Training of the 3rd B, 126th Regt. proceeds.	
	20th		do	
	21st		O.C. 3rd B, 126th proceeds to course at 2nd Army School.	
	22nd		Bn. war billeys at NORTKELINGHEM	
			— do —	
	23rd		B. returns to NIELLES & continues training.	
	24th		Training continues — great scarcity of American officers	
			— do —	
	25th		— do —	
	26th		H.A.C. platoon gave a demonstration to 37 B, 126th Regt of attacking strong point.	
	27th		Training continues	
	28th		— do —	
	29th		— do —	
	30th		Warning order received that 26th American division might proceed East, at beginning of February.	J.M. Saunders Lt Col cmdg 6/R.Stafford Regt for Lt Col cmdg

www.ingramcontent.com/pod-product-compliance
Lightning Source LLC
Chambersburg PA
CBHW081545160426
43191CB00011B/1841